SINGLE-HANDED

SINGLE-HANDED:

Letters from the Front

Michael Hickey

Book Guild Publishing
Sussex, England

First Published in Great Britain in 2008 by
The Book Guild Ltd
Pavilion View
19 New Road
Brighton, BN1 1UF

Typesetting in Garamond by
Ellipsis Books Ltd, Glasgow

Printed in Great Britain by
CPI Antony Rowe

A catalogue record for this book is available from
The British Library.

ISBN 978 1 84624 225 0

CONTENTS

PREFACE

When the Dalgliesh family drew my attention to a hoard of letters and several sketchbooks that had languished for many years in an old suitcase, I found myself confronting a treasure trove. Kenneth Dalgliesh grew to manhood in the Edwardian age when correspondence with pen and ink was the normal method of communication. He emerges from his letters, and the short memoir he wrote for his family towards the end of his life, as very much a man of his time. He was devoted to his parents and to his Uncle Richard ('Uncle Dick'), an engineer and ironmaster, in whose household at Asfordby near Melton Mowbray he spent many summer holidays, affectionately describing with a keenly observant eye the lives lived by all classes in late Victorian and Edwardian rural Leicestershire.

Kenneth was a good draughtsman, taking his sketchbooks with him to the trenches and later to Egypt. Whether drawing the Flanders farms in which he and his men were billeted, the sheer squalor of life in the trenches, his fellow officers, or the ancient ruins of the lower Nile valley, his drawings have an immediacy denied the camera. He emerges as a humane leader, caring for his men in an exemplary manner as they all struggled to pick up the soldier's trade under appalling conditions. His time at the Front was all too short, for a German sniper deprived him of his left arm on the slopes of Messines Ridge.

The loss of a limb did not deter Kenneth Dalgliesh from further military service and he spent the rest of the war censoring the mails in Egypt. His artistic gifts, and ability to describe all he saw there (together with his delightfully sensitive account of his courtship of the nursing sister whose unromantic task it was to treat his Nile Boils), give a fascinating insight into the lives of a generation now departed but to which we all owe an immeasurable debt of gratitude.

In later life Dalgliesh became distinguished in his profession, helped his beloved wife bring up a handsome and gifted family, and played a full part in the life of his community. Although my name appears as the author of this book, it is really his work. I count myself privileged to have been entrusted by the family with its editorship.

Kenneth's son, David, and Cally his wife have never failed in their hospitality and help. Their son Adam and daughter, Anna Kastanias, took the trouble to visit St Leonard's on Sea to photograph Marine Court, Kenneth's greatest architectural achievement. Jean Braithwaite, his daughter, who sent me an affectionate memoir of her parents, and Alex Wieck, his granddaughter, have also been of great assistance for which I am most grateful. The Dalgliesh family are most grateful to Greg Taylor for his expertise in photographing Kenneth Dalgliesh's sketchbooks.

Kenneth's old regiment, the Royal Leicesters, were merged into the Royal Anglian Regiment many years ago but The Royal Tigers' Association still thrives, thanks to the devotion of old comrades who jealously guard the identity and unquenchable spirit of their regiment. Their President, Major General Tony Pollard, has kindly written the Foreword. Chairman Bob Allan, Richard Lane, Regimental Historian, and Simon Jenkins, Head Curator, Leicestershire Record Office have gone out of their way to ensure I received all that I asked of them. I thank them most fervently.

Michael Hickey
Kintbury, West Berkshire, 2007

FOREWORD

By Major General A.J.G. Pollard, CB, CBE, DL
President, The Royal Tigers' Association

I was tempted when writing this foreword to follow the guiding
principle of the Royal Leicestershire Regiment's museum, which is
to display: 'ordinary men – extraordinary lives'. This seemed to apply
to Kenneth Dalgliesh, a young architect, and the subject of this
book, who served in the regiment. However, as I read I realised
that by any standards, and certainly by today's standards, Kenneth
Dalgliesh was no ordinary man. He was, like all of his generation
faced by the First World War, determined to serve King and Country,
to get to the Front, to do his duty. Seriously wounded and losing
an arm, Dalgliesh was still resolved to serve on in whatever capacity
he could.

Now, 90 years later, it is only a series of happy chances that have
combined to allow this book to come into existence. First, Kenneth
Dalgliesh was a most diligent, prolific and observant letter writer,
note maker and sketcher. Second, that he survived the Great War
at all was because he received his serious wounds just weeks before
his battalion, 1st/4th Leicesters, was virtually destroyed at Hohenzollern
Redoubt, where all the officers were casualties. Third, the Dalgliesh
family has since then carefully guarded his records. And finally, the
Dalgliesh family has found in Michael Hickey an author and editor
with a deep knowledge of military affairs and a strong and sympa-
thetic desire to make this story known.

From this combination of chances springs *Single-handed*, which
tells the story of a young man's experiences, from his childhood,

through his service in the Great War, to the effects this had on him for the rest of his life. The story, because it is largely told through extracts from his many, many letters home, is still extraordinarily fresh, since it is told in the first person and often in the present tense. From the pages shine Dalgliesh's desire to keep his parents free from worrying about him, his devotion to his soldiers, his high spirits and his almost matter-of-fact acceptance that he has lost his arm. What is also clear is his determination that he will be as little affected by this as possible and that there are still duties he can fulfil.

However, all is not that simple, because what starts as a tale of 'going to war' and of high hopes muddied by the dreadful events of life at the Front, becomes inexorably, page by page, a love story. Again the events that led to the partly disabled Kenneth Dalgliesh being sent to serve in Egypt as a Censor, also led him into contact with 'Sister', a nurse of remarkable devotion, herself with an unusually distinguished war record. And the charm of the tale again lies in the fact that, despite the passing of almost a century, it is told in the first person, to devoted parents, with all the breathless enthusiasm and delight that a young man can feel on falling in love.

This is a book about sense of duty, about rising above problems, about putting others first and about refusal to be frustrated by circumstances. Not qualities always rewarded today. It is told against the backdrop of the bitterly fought Great War, when the world was changing. It provides glimpses of Victorian life, of the Army's difficult transformation from all regular into a citizen's Army, of a son's love for his parents, 'My dear old people . . .', and of his falling in love with the woman with whom he was to share his life: 'Sister is dearer to me every day'.

Single-handed is also a factual account of events, unblurred by fiction and all the more moving for that. Such was the determination of Kenneth Dalgliesh that he was again commissioned in the Second World War, having already developed into a distinguished architect, some of whose buildings are today 'listed'. All of which tells us:

'extraordinary man – extraordinary life'; indeed, a man to whom the young can still look up and seek to emulate. Kenneth Dalgliesh's story is in its own way heroic, although he would undoubtedly have denied it.

Tony Pollard

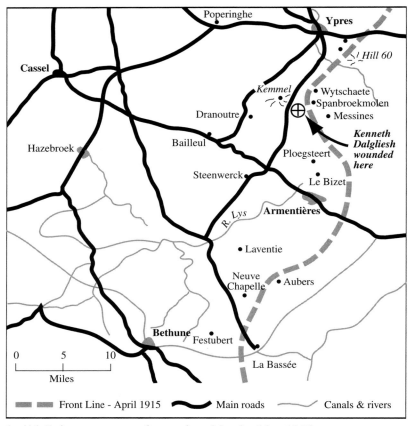

1st/4th Leicesters - area of operations March - May 1915

INTRODUCTION

This is the story of a man and a woman brought together by the fortunes of war. As such it is not unique, for there were countless similar romances during the war of 1914–1918, the watershed of our national history that changed forever the lives of millions together with the character and social structure of our country.

Those who survived would carry to their graves strong images of that seemingly endless golden summer of 1914 and a society which whilst far from perfect, was that of a nation confident in its mission under an essentially pacifist Liberal government, at the centre of a great Empire. As war clouds built up, the British people, seemingly unconcerned, carried on with their lives; Liberal politician Lloyd George raged against what he saw as the 'organised insanity' of the arms build-up in Europe. Doctors at London's Middlesex Hospital claimed to have treated cancer patients successfully with radium. Prime Minister Herbert Asquith rejected a Bill for the introduction of compulsory military service in the teeth of vigorous lobbying by the venerable Field Marshal Lord Roberts and his supporters. They had been urging the introduction of conscription, aware as they were of the mounting threat of Continental war and the resultant imperative for large, rapidly mobilised trained forces like those possessed by all the major European powers.

Mrs Emmeline Pankhurst and her two personable daughters Christabel and Sylvia were repeatedly arrested as leaders of the Suffragette movement for women's votes, as were many of their supporters, one of whom had died throwing herself in front of the King's horse in the 1913 Derby. The sternly Protestant Ulster

1

Volunteers, backed by Sir Edward Carson and a number of prominent Conservative politicians, had already recruited 100,000 men, illegally armed and training to resist any attempt by Westminster to impose Home Rule for a united Ireland against the wishes of the Protestant majority in the Six Counties. An unexpected bonus was the rapidity with which the Volunteers' membership responded to Kitchener's call for volunteers in the autumn to form the cadre of the superb 36th Infantry Division. Consisting of 'New Army' battalions of those Irish regiments recruiting in the Protestant north they were destined to perish in their thousands on the first day of the Somme, July 1916.

Winston Churchill as First Lord of the Admiralty presented a naval budget over £2.5 million in excess of the previous one, to boost oil reserves and speed the battleship-building programme (he was also denounced by Carson, the Ulster Protestant leader, for deploying the 3rd Battle Squadron in northern Irish waters as a deterrent to the Ulster Volunteers' activities). Over 70 British officers stationed at the Curragh cavalry base outside Dublin tendered their resignations rather than obey any orders to move against the Protestants in the north.

The usual sporting and social occasions of the season took place as a confident and apparently immutable society went through its accustomed rituals: the Derby (won by Durbar II), Royal Ascot, Henley Royal Regatta, the Eton-Harrow match. By the end of July the season in London was over. In his old age the Jewish publisher Victor Gollancz would recall the hot summer nights when Oxford undergraduates like himself would sleep out in Christ Church Meadows under the old city walls. The annual programme of receptions and balls launched another year's crop of debutantes onto the marriage market and all with a mind to do so prepared to move north to the grouse moors for the Glorious Twelfth.

On the Continent, however, following the assassinations of the Archduke Franz Ferdinand and his wife at Sarajevo on 28 June, the crisis was boiling; Serbia mobilised on 26 July, one day before the Austrians invaded. A day later Russia began to mobilise as an ally of

France and Britain. France had already begun to call reservists back to the colours. The three governments were bound into alliances by treaty and Britain was pledged to go to the assistance of Belgium if she were to be invaded by Germany, as now seemed imminent. The dreadful realisation that war was about to break out came belatedly to a population unaccustomed to their country's physical involvement in European affairs. Whilst the Central Powers, Germany and Austria-Hungary, could rapidly mobilise a total of some 7.2 million men, and France about 4 million, Britain, which had long shrunk from the idea of compulsory military service, could only field its regular troops and their reservists, a total of just under 1 million, for service overseas. The Territorial Force, created as recently as 1907 for Home Defence by a merger of the old Volunteers and the Yeomanry, was only available for service within the United Kingdom. Russia, our other ally, had vast manpower resources – some 5 million – but would be slow to mobilise.

In the first days of August the die was cast; the British fleet mobilised on the 2nd as Germany declared war on France, and Britain declared its adherence to the treaty of 1839 guaranteeing the neutrality of Belgium, as German troops crossed the Belgian border on the 4th. Late that evening Britain was at war with Imperial Germany.

As the result of secret staff talks several years earlier between the War Office and the French High Command, a British Expeditionary Force, the BEF, had been prepared to meet the contingencies of the invasions of France and Belgium, should these occur. This force, consisting of two army corps and a cavalry division with supporting artillery, engineers and logistic units, was ashore in France between the 17th and 20th of the month and soon in action on Belgian soil. Apart from regular units recalled from all parts of the globe to form a further infantry division, these and the relatively small numbers of regular reservists were the only professional elements of the British Army. Once expended there were no fully-trained men to fill their places.

Kitchener, the national hero newly appointed as War Minister, was the first member of the Cabinet to appreciate the peril and called for volunteers for 'New Armies'. He did so deliberately rather than implement a huge expansion of the Territorial Force. Apart from the fact that he had a low opinion of the Territorials, considering them little more than enthusiastic amateurs, they were constitutionally bound to the role of Home Defence and could not be ordered overseas. Kitchener foresaw a long war, unlike the majority of his compatriots who fondly imagined it would be 'over by Christmas'. Realising that the recruitment, equipment and training of effective New Armies would take at least a year, he swallowed his pride and invited members of the Territorial Force to volunteer as individuals for overseas service. The great majority, to their eternal credit, did so. It was clear that the regular Army's manpower would be exhausted within months if not weeks as fighting intensified on the Western Front. Territorial units were soon fighting in France and Belgium, while others went abroad to replace regular garrisons brought home from around the Empire.

By the autumn of 1915 it was clear that the implementation of Kitchener's plans for rapid expansion of the Army had revealed serious weaknesses, due to the government's reluctance to prepare for what many experts had predicted: the inevitable involvement of Great Britain in a large-scale Continental war. Tens of thousands of officers and men in the New Armies and the Territorial Force were to pay a terrible price as a consequence.

Following the disastrous failure of the British offensive in the Battle of Loos in September 1915 an official report would criticise the failure of the War Office, in the person of its Minister, Lord Kitchener, to husband the trained manpower of the regular Army by using it to train the New Armies and also to provide the solid backbone for hastily raised New Army units whose officers and NCOs, however enthusiastic, were as raw as the men they commanded. The official historian went so far as to state, in his preface to the volume dealing with the campaigns of 1915:

The awful slaughter and pitiably small results of the battles of 1915 were the inevitable consequence of using inexperienced and partly trained officers and men to do the work of soldiers, and to do it with wholly insufficient material and technical equipment. The British nation had failed to keep up an adequate force, and had neglected to make reasonable preparations for war, in particular to provide for rapid expansion . . .

The narrative which follows, describing the mobilisation of a Territorial battalion of the Leicestershire Regiment, its baptism of fire on the Western Front in the spring of 1915, and the experiences of one of its junior officers, will serve to bear this out.

1

A VICTORIAN BOYHOOD

Kenneth Dalgliesh was born in 1887. On leaving Nottingham High School he decided to be an architect and was articled in 1905 to a Mr Richard Hill, who had been at one time Chief Assistant to the great Isambard Kingdom Brunel, creator of the broad gauge Great Western Railway among many other groundbreaking achievements. Kenneth went to London to begin his apprenticeship. At that time, horse-drawn as well as motor omnibuses plied the streets and Lord Rothschild gave braces of pheasants to their drivers at Christmas, to be proudly displayed by the driver's seat on every red omnibus. Little would those drivers have guessed that within weeks of the outbreak of war in 1914 they and their buses would be in France as troop carriers at the Front.

Mr Hill was a first-class teacher, and Kenneth duly qualified as an Associate of the Royal Institute of British Architects (ARIBA) in 1913. Before this, he had been brought up in a typical middle-class family of the late Victorian age and thoroughly immersed in its conventions and values.

The Dalglieshes could trace their descent back through William Turner Dalgliesh (1767–1845), a Master Mariner and great friend of John Paul Jones (1747–1792) who, after an exciting career as Master of a slaving ship, waged war as a privateer against British seaborne trade. William Turner fathered no less than 11 children by Susannah, his wife, of whom the seventh, David, was born in 1804; he was Kenneth's grandfather. Theodore Irving Dalgliesh, David's son, was born on 1 February 1855 and became an engraver in an age before the development of photogravure, when his highly skilled craft was essential for the illustration of pictorial magazines such as the *Illustrated London News* and the *Graphic* as well as for important professional and official documents. Theodore was at the forefront of his profession and became the Royal Engraver, entitled to the suffix of 'RE' after his name. In this capacity he engraved numerous court and state documents and proclamations. His son Kenneth inherited his skill as a draughtsman and would put this to good use when training his men for trench warfare and the construction of fieldworks, as well as when creating the delightful sketches he made in Belgium and Egypt during the war.

Theodore's elder brother Richard, known in the family as 'Uncle Dick', was born in 1844 and lived until 1922. His career compassed an age of considerable social mobility, an outstanding example being Field Marshal Sir William Robertson, the first (and still the only) soldier to rise from the rank of Private to be the professional head of the British Army as Chief of the Imperial General Staff 1915–1918. Richard Dalgliesh was a professional engineer, working for the old Midland Railway company. While engaged in preliminary surveys for the boring of the Doveholes Tunnel in Derbyshire he came across a rich deposit of ironstone. An instinctive entrepreneur and aware of its potential, he bought up the surrounding land, exploiting it to make a fortune, first as founding director of the Holwell Iron Company, whose foundries were established near Melton Mowbray, then of the great Stanton Ironworks into which it merged. He later became a benefactor of Melton Mowbray Hospital, the Royal National Lifeboat Institution (RNLI) and numerous other charities. By the end of his life he was something of a local grandee: Companion of the Bath (CB); a Deputy Lieutenant (DL) of the County of Leicester; and a Justice of the Peace (JP), and Honorary Colonel of Kenneth's old Battalion the 4th Leicesters.

Shortly after founding the Holwell company Uncle Dick went to live in the village of Asfordby, between Leicester and Melton, where he bought an old red brick farmhouse conveniently close to his iron works. The house was progressively enlarged as he grew more prosperous, by the addition of extra wings later described by his admiring

Richard Dalgliesh ('Uncle Dick'), left, in conversation with Captain Forrester, Master of the Quorn Hounds, in 1909. By this time Richard had made his fortune in the iron and steel industry and was a magistrate and Deputy Lieutenant of Leicestershire. Later he would serve a term as High Sheriff. His generosity enabled Kenneth to make a very successful career as an architect in the years following World War One.

Rough Trench with entrenching tool. (Temporary cover)

In the absence of official training pamphlets, Kenneth was obliged to use his draughtsman's skills to produce diagrams from which he could instruct his equally inexperienced men at Leicester in the autumnn of 1914. He did so by picking the brains of officers who had already served in France and Flanders. However, when the 1st/4th Leicesters arrived on the front line it was to find that they could not dig below three feet due to the saturated condition of the ground below Messines Ridge.

Trenches at Stoughton; shewing testing Hole. Dug by Service Company. Nov. 1914.

10

nephew as 'each more architecturally hideous than the last and terminated by an orangery in which he grew palms . . .'. It was a typical expression of high Victorian prosperity, characteristic of so many families of sound yeoman stock as they gained confidence in creating the nation's wealth and flexing their social muscles. Kenneth spent much of his youth there, recording those days in a memoir he wrote late in life for the benefit of his own family. In this he describes a way of life that was soon to vanish forever. At Asfordby he learned to fish, ride and play his part in the passage of the seasons in an English village.

He was sent to Nottingham High School in 1901. Whilst it offered a sound education and was the best that Kenneth's parents could afford, he did not enjoy his time there. A number of relatives, including some kindly aunts, lived in Nottingham and provided some compensations, but Kenneth was homesick, missing his parents and pining for summer holidays at Asfordby with Uncle Dick. Looking back many years later he was to write:

My school years at Nottingham were an imprisonment to me, home and the family union meant so much and I would count the days to my liberation each term. Don't think I was completely miserable, for the family I lived with were kind . . . the school I frankly didn't like. I was sensitive and it was rough . . .

However, there was always the prospect of holidays at Asfordby:

There was a bridge over the river leading to the paddocks where the brood mares and the yearlings grazed. It was by this bridge that I caught my first fish, a beautiful roach. I shall never forget the thrill of feeling that fish on my line. It was also here, in the paddock, that the annual village flower show was held – the event of the year. Big marquees smelling as only marquees can smell, the vegetables and flowers all so beautifully laid out. Swing boats, coconut shies, shooting galleries, and of course the village policeman. Lovely ladies gowned as only the Edwardians knew how to gown a woman, lace and satin petticoats, parasols and wonderful hats ...women were magnificent in that era from the youngest maid to the oldest dowager ...

Elsewhere on the estate lay other delights:

The stables consisted of the old farm stalls and saddle room, to which my uncle had added a coach house and loose box ... there was also a pigsty on the wall of which I loved to stand with a long willow wand and make the pigs gallop round ... I can see and smell it all and they were good stable smells, especially the saddle room with its harness, burnished bits, and carriage whips. There was also another smell, that of the hay and the carrots which I was told made the horses' coats glossy ... The groom's name was Willie Tyler and the under-groom was Johnny Prior. William was a fine character, every inch a coachman, so much so that when he was driving the carriage and saw his old father on the road he would never move a muscle but look straight ahead, while the old man stood respectfully by the roadside and touched his hat to the 'gentry'. William was my friend through life, I went to see him when he lay dying in his cottage and I followed him down the village street with an aching heart when his coffin was reverently carried on the shoulders of four friends to the old village churchyard. God rest his soul; he was a man.

Uncle Dick, the industrial magnate, ran his company like some Russian autocrat, as Kenneth vividly recalled:

He was a violent-tempered man, but always kind to me. He had a very short and effective way of dealing with labour disputes. One day a deputation headed by 'Darky Smith' came to the office to lodge a complaint. He got up from his desk, took off his jacket, rolled up his sleeves and went out to meet the deputation. Asking for the spokesman he informed him that he was the manager and as such would manage the works in his way, and thereupon 'squared up'. Darky had no alternative but to accept the challenge and got a good hiding for his trouble. The deputation then returned to their allotted tasks, sadder but wiser men.

Richard Dalgliesh may have been a hard man, but half a century before the welfare state he ensured that unemployment was virtually non-existent in the village and that his employees were decently housed. His outside staff included two gardeners:

Freddy Prime who preached in the local chapel on Sundays (my uncle referred to him as 'one of the long-eared gentry') and old Clinch, who always walked with his arms behind him as if he were pulling an invisible barrow. His stock remark was that 'it will be a terrible fine wet day, Master'. I never could think of the correct answer to this somewhat cryptic remark.

In the winter time I spent a large part of the day indoors . . . if the coast was clear I would slip quietly into the larder and pick small crumbs from the Leicester cheese of which I was inordinately fond, and smell the bread . . . another place I loved to visit was my uncle's wine cellar, not for any material reward but more for excitement. On Sunday mornings he would summon his eldest daughter and the housekeeper and proceed, with myself at a discreet distance, to the cellar to select a bottle of port. After much consideration one was chosen and carried out with as much care as if it had been his first-born, accompanied by vitriolic injunctions not to shake it, such as 'Damn your eyes – look where you're going'. The cork was reverently drawn and the bottle duly sampled, when it would either be passed as satisfactory or relegated to the kitchen for cooking and I would fly for my life with such remarks as 'Corked, by God!' ringing in my ears . . .

quietly down a lane. I love to hear the Huntsman talking to them and calling them individually by name – Bugler, Lady, Music and Captain . . .

In an era when social cohesion had not been scattered to the winds by two world wars and the toppling of a seemingly immutable social order, the rural week centred around a Sabbath which, though not observed with Pharisaical zeal except by the stricter dissenting sects, nevertheless united all classes in churchgoing. The Anglican Church, amply provided with well educated graduate clergy, still enjoyed a high level of prestige, social status and confidence in itself. Children were brought up to a habit of regular attendance from an early age, with emphasis on the offices of matins and evensong. Regular attendance at Sunday School ensured that they possessed a sound knowledge of the scriptures and of the incomparable language of the King James Bible and Book of Common Prayer. Before their confirmation they would be methodically catechised. Holy Communion, at least in rural areas, was regarded as an act of intensely personal worship and had yet to be seen as the central corporate act of the church's week although, as bidden in the rubrics of the Church of England, Easter was recognised as the principal day of obligation, and three attendances at Holy Communion during the Church's year were seen as the decent norm. Kenneth's views on church were certainly typical of the young of his generation:

Sundays were good days in my eyes. People seemed to have more time to spare for my particular entertainment. My aunt always went to church 'douce honest woman' and took me, and I thoroughly enjoyed it as there was so much to see. Tom the miller sang in the choir, Billy Hands blew the organ, there was the cripple who had to be helped into his seat, William's old father, and a whole crowd of friends. Billy was a kindly simpleton; the story goes that when he was a boy the house was struck by lightning and his brother was killed alongside him in bed, and Billy suffered a defect in his speech ever after. I could imitate him quite well though I was careful not to do so as he was numbered among my friends. It was in that old church, with its smell of hassocks and oil lamps, that I learned to know the lovely old chants and hymn tunes, which linger with one through life. It is a pity that so many parsons have lost their hold on the people; one may not have understood all that was said and done, but one experienced a sense of peace and happiness there and gradually came to know that there were such things in the Prayer Book as the 21st Psalm . . .

Life in a rural community at the end of the nineteenth century was anything but serene and could be one of worry and grinding hard labour for the poorer classes, unprotected as they were by comprehensive welfare and medical legislation. The welfare state was still half a century distant, and the spectre of the Union Workhouse, where life was made as uncongenial as possible for the able-bodied poor and where aged married couples could be separated, was a strong incentive to find work of any kind, however ill paid. Kenneth, sensitive to the problems faced by the villagers of Asfordby, closely observed the characters around him:

There was Johnny Underwood who mended the roads – he stood about four foot high and was somewhat cantankerous; Ellen Back who always wore men's corduroys and smoked a clay pipe; Benny the Moulder who taught me how to fish; Sammy Tyres the carter who would let me ride his trace horse or drive his cart; and Sally Rowton whose old father was the village baker and kept the sweet shop. What a wonderful little shop it was, smelling of warm bread. I can still hear the tinkle of the door bell and see the jars of sweets in the window – bulls' eyes, pink and white hearts with mottos on them, yards of liquorice laces (I must have eaten several miles!), bars of Fry's chocolate in wooden boxes. There were also tallow candles hanging in bunches from the low ceiling. Sally was somewhat of a village belle and usually served the customers as her old father was very deaf and would lean over the counter with his ear cupped in his hand and even then he seldom heard what was said . . . all is changed now, my old friends are dead and the old house and garden split up into cottage property. I should not like to see it again.

2

AT THE THRESHOLD

In the last years of peace before the world went to war, young men like Kenneth, nearing their professional qualifications and keen to break out from the bonds of apprenticeship, were invariably short of funds; his father was not wealthy and had to inform his son that his allowance would have to be ended:

> Strange to say, this was no shock to me, but instead it infused in me a sense of great elation. I was my own master and must stand or fall by my own efforts. I was through my articles of pupillage and had come to understand and love my work and was once again filled with ambition . . .

A popular form of recreation for young bachelors working in London was to go dancing, for which they were required to don white tie and tails. One of Kenneth's friends managed

> . . . the miraculous feat of changing into his dress clothes in a hansom cab, so as not to be late, for in those days there were little pink, blue and white programmes with pencils attached by a silk cord and tassel and if one was late all the 'pick of the bunch' would be booked and one would have to fall back on the 'wallflowers'. Dancing was more strenuous then as you will discover if the Lancers are revived.

In the summer of 1914, newly qualified as an architect, Kenneth decided to widen his horizons before settling down in his profession, and signed on as Purser aboard a tramp steamer, one of hundreds then plying the seas for custom under the Red Ensign, carrying almost any form of cargo to wherever the shipping agents could obtain contracts. On this voyage the ship carried a cargo of best Welsh steam coal out of Cardiff, bound for Spain. Hugging the coast after a stormy passage through the Bay of Biscay, it passed through the Straits of Gibraltar and reached Valencia, its destination, on 2 August. By now rumours of impending war were rife and it was known that the German battle cruiser *Goeben* and her escort, the cruiser *Breslau*, were at large in the western Mediterranean, where they made a surprise attack on the French north African ports on the following day, the first act of the sea war against the *entente cordiale*. Kenneth's ship remained at Valencia for over a week until the immediate danger had evaporated (the two German warships, ineffectually pursued by the British Mediterranean Fleet, had made for Constantinople where they were transferred to the Ottoman Navy). On 12 August the tramp left for England with a cargo of oranges and lemons, arriving at London Docks a week later. Within 24 hours Kenneth and one of his friends were trying to enlist, to be told that all the City territorial units were over-subscribed; but thanks to the influence of Uncle Dick, who was Chairman of the Leicestershire Territorial Association, Kenneth was commissioned into the Leicesters. As a preliminary he would have had to complete Army Form E536: 'Questions to be Answered by a Candidate for Appointment to a Commission in the Territorial Force'. Having expressed his wish to serve in the Leicestershire Regiment he had to specify the battalion, in this case the 4th, and the rank ('Sec Lieutenant') into which he hoped to be commissioned. He was required to answer a number of questions, some of which would be regarded with dismay in today's 'multicultural' society:

- Are you a British subject by birth or naturalisation?
- Are you of pure European descent?
- At what school or college were you educated?
- What is your height?

- Have you held a Commission, or are you now serving in any of His Majesty's Regular, Reserve, Territorial, Auxiliary, Indian or Colonial Forces, the Channel Islands Militia, or the Officers' Training Corps?

To most of these questions Kenneth was able to give affirmative replies and in particular his service in the Officers' Training Corps at school would assure the recruitment authorities that he possessed at least some military knowledge. As his parents were living in Kent, near Hythe, Uncle Dick, who endorsed Kenneth's application, was able to keep an avuncular eye on him as he embarked on his martial career.

The British Army of 1914 was unrecognisable from that of the twenty-first century. Its regular units were essentially an imperial gendarmerie organised, trained and equipped to police widely-flung outposts of Empire and in particular to keep the peace of the Raj in India, where civil unrest was always a possibility and insurgency among the fierce tribes of the North West Frontier called for ceaseless vigilance. Frequent punitive expeditions had to be mounted by ad hoc 'field forces' assembled for the purpose. The old frontier was a hard training school, calling for high standards of fitness, and recognition that the insurgent tribesmen were both brave and ruthless.

Until 1880 the Army was still recognisable as the one that had overcome Napoleon at Waterloo and blundered its way through the war in the Crimea in the 1850s – a collection of numbered infantry battalions. Drastically reorganised as the result of the so-called Cardwell Reforms, the numbered infantry regiments became two or more regular battalions with close territorial associations to the counties. Each regiment had its own depot, usually in a county town, in order to further the regional connection. The old 17th Foot had long been associated with the county of Leicestershire and had borne its territorial name as long ago as 1815. In 1880 this association was confirmed and the numeric title dropped when it became the Leicestershire Regiment. It had been raised in 1688 in the last months of the reign of King James II, bearing the name of its first Colonel, Solomon Richards. Its initial role was the defence of Windsor Castle, where it was on duty to greet King William III and Queen Mary, and to pledge loyalty to them and the House of Orange on their arrival there in 1689. Then it was deployed to the Netherlands, gaining its first battle honour at Namur in 1695. Thereafter it followed the typical pattern of all infantry regiments of the line, serving in Portugal (including the battle of Almanza where the British Army suffered defeat at the hands of James II's bastard son, the Catholic Duke of Berwick) and throughout the wars of the Spanish Succession. When regiments ceased to bear their Colonels' names, this one became the 17th of Foot in 1713 and in 1782, after long involvement on the American continent, its county association began, at least notionally. When it became the 17th Leicestershire Regiment, its Commanding Officers (COs) were urged to cultivate 'a connection with that county which might at all times be useful towards recruiting'. Although it played little part in the Napoleonic Wars, its extended service in India from 1804 to 1823 earned it the right, granted by King George IV in 1825, to bear on its colours a depiction of a Royal Tiger and the word 'Hindoostan'. These also featured on the regular battalion's cap badge (although for some obscure and mean-spirited reason the territorial battalions were denied the addition of the 'Hindoostan' honour scroll on theirs until after the start of the First World War). The Leicesters thus became known to generations of soldiers as 'The Tigers'. For most of the nineteenth century the regiment served in campaigns such as the annexation of Scinde (1838), the First Afghan War (1838–1842), the Crimean War, the Second Afghan War of 1880, and the wars in Burma resulting in the absorption of that country into the Indian Empire.

Whilst the regular component of the Army had spent much of the nineteenth century serving abroad, the need to protect the home country had exercised politicians who were, as ever, determined to achieve this at minimal cost. Following the Napoleonic Wars the old militia decayed until a fresh threat from France was perceived in the 1850s. This led to the construction of costly defensive works (known as 'Palmerston's Follies') guarding Portsmouth and the approaches to London, and the revival of the home defence forces in the form of the Volunteers and, as the cavalry arm, the Yeomanry. Whether on foot or mounted these were of variable military worth but at least they gave good citizens the chance to don uniform (and incidentally to buttress their real or imaginary social standing). Beginning in 1905 the Liberal government's gifted War Minister, Richard Haldane, presided over a drastic reform of the Volunteers to create the Territorial Force. Each county regiment was allotted its Territorial battalions, the number of which depended on the size of a county's population. Haldane also overhauled the Army's staff system, creating a rigorously selected and trained General Staff on the lines of the Prussian model, which he greatly admired. The very existence of this, expanded into the Imperial General Staff in order to coordinate the land forces of the Empire, was instrumental in the prompt mobilisation and despatch to France of the BEF within days of the outbreak of war. However, the unforeseen rate of attrition encountered in the first months of combat quickly made it apparent that Britain was not prepared to wage an extended Continental war.

On the outbreak of war the Leicesters had two Regular battalions (1st and 2nd), a Militia or Special Reserve battalion (the 3rd, which was little more than a holding unit for the provision of personnel), and two Territorial battalions: the 4th, recruited within the city of Leicester, and the 5th, which drew its members from around the county and whose company drill halls were located in the larger market towns. Both these units, thanks to local connections, were close-knit. In the Officers' Mess, local company and factory managers, professional men and landowners predominated; serving in the ranks were many of the men who worked in their officers' firms and businesses. Overseers, skilled artisans and foremen were natural choices for promotion into the Warrant Officers' and Sergeants' Mess and the working relationship was carried into the Saturday drill nights and summer camps, which drew from some regulars the somewhat dismissive description of the Territorials as 'weekend warriors' or 'Saturday night soldiers'. Notwithstanding such slurs, the 4th Leicesters enjoyed a strong team identity and all ranks knew that their performance on active service, should the need arise, would be sedulously reported home in letters, a factor that encouraged all to give of their best. There was however a fairly high peacetime turnover rate of personnel in both Territorial battalions, as some who joined soon tired of the discipline while others, resenting the way in which the hierarchy of the workplace was still observed when in uniform, left the Territorials after a few months.

While the depot of the Leicesters' Regular battalions and regimental headquarters was at Glen Parva Barracks outside the city, the old Magazine in the city centre, with its imposing gatehouse, was the headquarters of the 4th Battalion. The gatehouse had originally formed part of an ambitious medieval religious charitable foundation including a collegiate church and almshouses, founded in 1330 just outside the city walls by Henry, Earl of Lancaster. This institution was suppressed in the reign of Henry VIII and fell into decay, apart from the gatehouse which, by 1642, at the beginning of the Civil War, had become the city magazine, thus acquiring the name it still bears. By the early nineteenth century it had regained its military association, and new barracks for the county militia were built to replace the ruins of the old collegiate establishment. It is clear from his subsequent letters that Kenneth was proud to become a 'Tiger', welcomed into an illustrious regiment that had marched under the great Duke of Marlborough.

Appointments to commissions in the Territorial Force were granted by His Majesty the King – in this case George V, '. . . through orders under the Secretary of State or by regulation'. A potential officer candidate initially recommended by the President of the County Territorial Association would normally be appointed to the lowest commissioned rank of Second Lieutenant within 30 days of the CO's notification of a vacancy in the battalion. Such candidates were required, somewhat vaguely, to possess 'qualifications recognised' (but not specified) by the regulations. These could include passing the Certificate 'A' of the Officers' Training Corps, units of which could be found in most if not all public and grammar schools. Potential officers had to be at least 17 years of age; no examination was required, and the candidature had to be approved by the King or his representative. Kenneth had the backing of Uncle Dick, widely known and respected as its Chairman by the influential men who served on the County Territorial Association Committee. As soon as his commission had been confirmed he would be required to play a full part in the training of the battalion to which he was assigned, picking up the rudiments of soldiering as he went.

His first preoccupation was the purchase of uniform and accoutrements for which he received a grant of £20 from official funds. Under peacetime regulations this had to be returned if he failed to satisfy an examining board after two years. He then had to learn, as best he could, about military law, weapon training, map-reading,

Officers of the 2nd/4th Leicesters at the Magazine, in the autumn of 1914. Kenneth Dalgliesh is second from the right, back row. The measure of inexperience in this unit may be deduced from the lack of any campaign medal ribbons other than those worn by the commanding officer.

foot drill, ceremonial etiquette and – just as important – the etiquette of Mess life. As no officer cadet schools for non-regular officers existed in 1914, the onus lay squarely on the individual officer, supervised in Territorial units by his CO and Adjutant, the latter invariably a regular soldier, as was the unit Quartermaster. It was upon these, aided by their Permanent Staff Instructors (PSIs), all regular long-service Non-Commissioned Officers (NCOs) and Warrant Officers, and the commissioned Quartermaster, that the burden of mobilising the unit fell. On 5 August, while Kenneth, unaware of the declaration of war, was still fretting aboard his ship at Valencia, the scene at the Magazine would have resembled that of a disturbed ants' nest. On receipt of the War Office telegram 'Mobilise Troopers' a well-rehearsed sequence of staff drills would have taken place. All active members of the Territorial battalion were sent their mobilisation telegram and reported to battalion headquarters, to be joined within days by recalled regular reservists and in due course by new arrivals like Kenneth, to bring the battalion up to its war establishment of almost 1,000 officers and men. At the same time the 5th Battalion was mobilising at its drill halls around the county.

As there was insufficient room at the Magazine, the eight rifle companies of the 4th Battalion now occupied board, or council, schools in the city where their equipment was brought up to scale, nominal rolls made out, and reservists given medical examinations. Many would have to be rejected as hopelessly unfit for service and duly discharged with a £20 bounty. The battalion's transport was almost entirely horse- or mule-drawn, and provision was made in King's Regulations for the impressment of animals and vehicles. This involved the compulsory purchase of draught animals and officers' chargers (for Adjutants, Majors and COs) and was carried out with the assistance of veterinary officers and 'Inspectors of Remounts' – usually retired cavalry officers resident in the county, whose job was to examine the animals and, if found satisfactory, agree a fair price for all purchases. Many of the impressed vehicles were tradesmen's vans, which proved suitable for the carriage of small arms ammunition and unit stores. One baker's van, taken off the streets of Leicester, served with the regiment in France and Flanders before its return, somewhat battered, to its pre-war owner.

Before the battalion could deploy from the Magazine to its mobilisation location a great deal of administration and documentation had to be completed. Within days this had been achieved and the 4th Battalion entrained for Luton where the rest of the 46th North Midland Territorial Division was forming up prior to taking up its war role of Home Defence. In the absence of adequate barrack accommodation the troops had to be billeted on the local civilian population, a procedure for which King's Regulations were invoked. As in the case of impressed animals and vehicles, the government was bound by law to pay a fair rent or hire charge.

Having paraded to lay up their colours at St Martin's Church (now Leicester Cathedral), the 1st/4th Leicesters march back to the Magazine barracks through cheering crowds in pouring rain. (Photo: *Leicester Mercury*)

In field service marching order with full packs, the 1ˢᵗ/4ᵗʰ head for the railway station en route to their mobilisation location at Luton. The soldiers in the foreground are part of the Corps of Drums – men trained on bugle and fife. (Photo: *Leicester Mercury*)

On 12 August the results of a week's frantic effort were on display. The battalion paraded on the Magazine drill square under the eyes of its Honorary Colonel, the Duke of Rutland and his Duchess, both proudly watching their son, the Marquess of Granby, as he marched at the head of his platoon. The King's and regimental colours were laid up in accordance with King's Regulations in St Martin's Church and a few days later the battalion, in full field service marching order, trooped off to the railway station to entrain for Belper, where it remained for a short period before moving to Luton. The unit historian notes that it was an extremely hot day. The troops, distracted by the patriotic attentions of crowds lining the roadside, possibly affected by the amorous embraces and loyal potations thrust upon them from the crowd, and unaccustomed to marching heavily laden, found it hard to maintain their dressing in the ranks and to keep in step. Many of the general reservists recalled to the colours were medically sub-standard and fell out on the line of march. But the 4th Leicesters, however raw and inexperienced, were marching as to war and could get on with serious training as the unit shook down for its war role, shedding dozens of its more elderly personnel as clearly unfit for active service. On arrival at Luton most of the battalion was quartered in schools, private homes and dissenting chapels. The locals were friendly and hospitable. The town swarmed with soldiers as the division formed up, under the command of Major General Montague-Stuart-Wortley, who was keen to get to the Front in France as soon as possible, for like the rest of the country he probably believed that the war would be over by Christmas.

3

AN ARCHITECT UNDER ARMS

Kenneth had always written regularly to his parents, this being the convention when letters were the normal means of communication. His reflect membership of a close-knit and affectionate family, usually beginning 'My dear old family . . .' and typically signed off with 'Best of love, God bless you all, Ken'.

To cope with the patriotic surge of recruitment, Territorial units were spawning second battalions. The 1st Battalion of the 4th Leicesters, henceforth known as the 1st/4th, was at Luton, preparing for Home Defence, but all ranks were aware that it was likely to be sent overseas. Kenneth served his military apprenticeship at the Magazine in Leicester where the 2nd/4th Battalion, a 'Home Service' unit, was forming from personnel who, for family or business reasons, had felt unable to go overseas with the 1st Battalion, older reservists of lower medical categories, and drafts of enthusiastic recruits, all volunteers. Kenneth's first letter home from the Magazine is dated 12 October 1914, his first day as an officer, and reflects his trepidation at the responsibilities thrust upon him despite his lack of military knowledge:

. . . I caught the 7.50 to Leicester this morning and duly reported myself at the Magazine at 9.40. I was then sent off to the Racecourse with three other subalterns, where we found the battalion hard at work; between 500 & 600 men busy with physical drill. I was introduced to my Captain (Simpson) and strolled around till 10.30 when the battalion fell in for Company drill which lasted till we were dismissed at 12.30. I have been appointed to 'A' Company. My Captain doesn't appear to be exactly a favourite but he has been very nice to me so far. I am fortunate in having a couple of very smart Sergeants, one in particular is a priceless man, Sgt Connolly. I had a chat with him this morning and told him it was 10 years since I had done any drill, so if he saw me in a mess he was to come along and give me a hand. He said that was quite all right and he would help me all he could . . . this afternoon I was put in charge of a half company at 2.30 when we fell in, so I let my Sergeants do the work and kept my ears open! I wonder how I shall get on tomorrow! As I don't think I shall have an earthly chance of keeping a diary, will you keep my letters and I will endeavour to make them as much of a diary as possible.

Best of wishes dearest family, God bless you all, Ken.

With the willing support of his regular Sergeants, familiar to generations of raw Subalterns in all regiments, Kenneth grew in confidence, drilling his men and leading them on route marches. On 18 October he was able to write with growing confidence:

Dear old family,

I'm beginning to feel much more at home with the men now and take command of a half company regularly . . . Colonel Oliver was drilling the Battalion and being Company 'A' I had to march in front of the whole lot – a great responsibility as I hadn't anyone to watch!

We've had two route marches this week, one of five miles and one yesterday of eight miles. My feet are holding out wonderfully, they are of course very bruised . . . I gave them a soaking in boracic acid this morning . . .

During his eight-mile march there was a halt outside a village where Kenneth was confronted with indiscipline for the first time when some of the men ran off to the nearest pub; he sent after them and ordered them into close arrest. Somewhat lamely he adds:

> ... I don't know what their ultimate fate was, I was too tired to bother when we dismissed ...

Meanwhile his military education continued:

> On Friday we had a lecture (officers and NCOs) at the Magazine on how an officer should conduct himself in the field – very interesting indeed, the room was very hot and I could barely keep awake ...

In late October Kenneth was still at Leicester, living in 'diggs' (*sic*) with a family of Belgian refugees and reporting daily at the Magazine. He was seeing something of Uncle Dick, who was given to visiting him. Meanwhile at Luton the 46th North Midland Division underwent a series of close inspections by senior officers, first by General Sir Ian Hamilton the Commander in Chief Home Forces, then by Lord Kitchener the War Minister who, despite his known antipathy towards the Territorial Force, knew that it would have to be sent to France to fill the gaps in the line while the 'New Army' of men responding to his call for volunteers was being kitted out and trained from scratch for active service. As yet there was no suggestion that conscription be introduced and Kitchener continued to supervise an army of volunteers, albeit of three different categories: the Regular element, now gravely depleted as the result of heavy casualties suffered in the earlier battles; the Territorials, already filling gaps in the line, and now the New Army units, condemned to appalling conditions in makeshift camps all over Britain, training as best they could under elderly NCOs and officers and with wholly inadequate equipment. Many units still lacked proper uniforms and tentage as late as November 1914. Following his inspection of the 46th Division Kitchener told Stuart-Wortley that it could not be sent overseas until a second-line division had been trained to take its place for Home

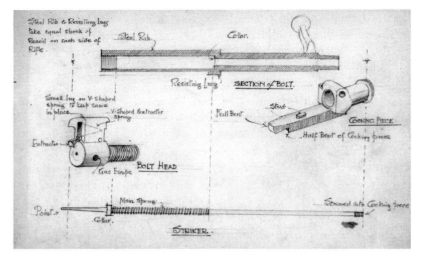

Presumably due to shortage (or absence) of official training manuals, 2/Lt Dalgliesh used his draughtsman's skills to produce his own aids for weapon training in the autumn of 1914.

Defence. Then the whole division marched past, as Kitchener took the salute. In the words of the 4th Leicesters' Battalion historian, expressing a spectator's view:

> What a sight it was, a glittering sea of bayonets, wave after wave of sombre khaki, battalion after battalion, brigade after brigade, interspersed with well-mounted commanding officers, spruce keen-eyed adjutants, waxed-moustached sergeant majors looking exceeding fierce. The cream of the manhood of the Midlands was here, big sunburnt men, all fighting fit ... a division at war strength is an awe-inspiring sight ... every man with a glint of battle in his eye and straining at the leash to get his hands on his country's foes, a sight for the gods ... [as the historian was right to add, the mood in the ranks was actually somewhat different] ... having been under arms for four and a half hours, the battalion marches

past in quarter column, a seething mass of suppressed profanity, stifled curses . . . the men in the ranks jostle each other, elbows delve into ribs, and toes are trodden on but everybody is doing his best . . .

Kenneth's passion for gardening was rewarded in October 1914 by his winning a cash prize in the *Country Life* gardens competition, reported in a letter of the 29th of that month describing how he spent the money – on a framed photographic portrait of himself in uniform and a book on *Houses and Gardens* by Lutyens. His enthusiasm for soldiering, his pride of regiment and abundant high spirits are evident as he describes how he is determined to get his inexperienced men up to 'guards' standard'. At this point, many Territorial units were being invited to volunteer for overseas service. The Territorial Force was constitutionally designated for Home Service only, but appalling casualties incurred by the BEF in France and Flanders required urgent reinforcement. Territorial battalions were immediately despatched to plug the gaps in the line, notably at Ypres. For the time being, however, the 1st/4th Leicesters continued to train at Luton. Kenneth, still training recruits at the Magazine, had not yet been formally gazetted as a Second Lieutenant and was beginning to hanker after the back pay due to him; his weekly rent bill for his 'diggs' was 23 shillings and he was presumably reliant on savings, or whatever financial help his family could provide. For their part, they helped with gifts such as the offer of handkerchiefs, for which he thanked them: '. . . yes, I should like some, only they must be khaki; white ones are not allowed on active service'. He was careful not to alarm his parents by expressing his frustration at remaining at the Magazine with the 2nd/4th when the 1st/4th Battalion was clearly approaching operational efficiency, justifying its despatch to France with the rest of the 46th Division.

By early November he had at last been gazetted and had received the handkerchiefs ('. . . they look most awfully nice . . .'). Route marches were now more demanding, and meanwhile the 1st/4th Battalion had moved from Luton to Bishops Stortford. Back at the

Magazine, Kenneth was still training recruits before sending them on as drafts to the $1^{st}/4^{th}$ when up to standard. At the same time he too was learning his trade as a soldier, in particular the difficult art of man-management. Sensing laxity in the men, who had been talking and swearing on the line of march, he took them to the side of the parade ground and

> . . . had a quiet talk to them . . . I told them plainly that my ambition was to have 'A' Company the smartest in the battalion, and I was quite sure it was their ambition as well – they might do anything they bally well pleased off duty, but on parade it must be like clockwork. I didn't want to be on their backs for this that or the other, but I insisted on discipline *to the last letter.* Oh, I had a real heart to heart talk with them . . . I think it did them good for they marched *well* afterwards.

He reports, after one route march, that a rate of over 140 paces to the minute was adopted going out and 140 coming back. Characters were emerging from the ranks of his company; one, known as 'Ginger' or 'Nogger', was evidently the company wit and licensed buffoon. The men sang spontaneously on the line of march and the unit was developing its own identity. Most of the men, recruited as they were from the city of Leicester, were now billeted out with their own families and slept at home when not on guard duties. Only a few dutymen and the Sergeant Major, Mr Withers, slept at the Magazine. In a letter dated 19 November Kenneth describes a solemn memorial parade service in St Martin's Church for Field Marshal Earl Roberts of Kandahar VC, who had died while visiting units of the Indian Army in France. 'Bobs', as he was universally known (and celebrated as such by Kipling) gained his VC in the Indian Mutiny, had distinguished himself in the Afghan campaign of 1880–1881 and later in South Africa where he was sent to sort things out in 1900 after General Buller's early reverses. Roberts had long agitated for universal military service, having foreseen the inevitability of a prolonged war involving British armies on the European mainland. Events were to prove him right; had Britain possessed such huge reserves of trained military manpower as the Continental powers, it would not have been necessary to resort, as did Kitchener in 1914, to appeals for tens of thousands of volunteers, who now had to be clad, housed, fed, equipped and trained from scratch while the Territorials filled gaps in the line.

As winter drew on, the battalion increased the intensity of its training with long route marches, 'field days' and practice in digging trench systems according to the latest Western Front doctrine; in this latter subject Kenneth was able to apply his architectural skills – his detailed drawings as instructional guides for his men, made with great precision and impeccable draughtsmanship, are small works of art. Practice of infantry tactics in open order was not neglected and alternated with trench-digging as part of the battalion's programme. Field firing – musketry carried out under more realistic conditions than on the rifle range – was undergone at Dunstable. In a letter dated 6 December Kenneth describes an extended three-day route march when his company, followed by its cooks and their wagon, marched all day, interspersed with field training, and bivouacked overnight. The second night bivouac was located on Uncle Dick's land at Asfordby; their host inspected the unit after breakfast and, to Kenneth's delight (and doubtless Uncle Dick's gratification), received three cheers for his hospitality. On its return to Leicester the company had marched 65 miles in three days with full packs. The men had good reason to be pleased with themselves; 'A' Company had become a confident and fit body of men, unrecognisable from the raw material of August. Morale was evidently high, and the men sang heartily on the march. The young officers were settling into the spirit of Mess life; Kenneth refers to their enjoyment of the card game euchre, and to the horseplay '. . . a bally old rag . . .' inevitable during a high-spirited dinner night. His pay was now '. . . about 10/6d a day and I'm still only paying 23/- a week for my digs . . .' Christmas was celebrated in the traditional way at the Magazine, the officers waiting on the men at the Christmas lunch and the traditional light-hearted football match between the Sergeants' and Officers' Messes. Most of the men would enjoy a second feast at their homes in Leicester.

The battalion was already acquiring its own *esprit*; the men – now fitter than they had ever been thanks to physical exercise and the robust diet of the cookhouse – marched with swagger and confidence whether on the parade ground or on extended route marches, when they indulged in their self-composed songs:

> *We are the Leicester boys,*
> *Yes we're the Leicester boys*
> *We know our manners*
> *We spend our tanners*
> *We're respected wherever we go.*
> *When you see us on parade*
> *Open your windows wide*
> *All the girls begin to cry*
> *I tiddly, I tiddly, Ayti ayti ayti I!*
> *We are the Leicester boys . . .*

Another marching song began '*When the beer's on the table we'll be there . . .*'.

The humour of the British soldier has endured through the Army's history and Kenneth warmed to that of his men in a postscript to a letter home on 3 November 1914:

The other day, Bibles and Prayer Books were served out. Directly afterwards the men were taken for a route march. On halting them by the side of the road for a rest the Subalterns went on some little distance to pace out some distances for j.d. [judging distance – part of the infantry training syllabus]. When they returned, the 'wit' of the company was found seated on the ground with a large circle of men round him, and all singing hymns! Going hammer and tongs!!

By the end of 1914 the battalion was reorganised from eight small rifle companies into four large ones, each of four platoons, as Kenneth explained to his parents in a letter of 24 January 1915:

> Each platoon is commanded by a Subaltern and there are two commanders to each double company. I was immediately given No. 1 platoon and so got my seniority. Simpson said he thought it had better be so because I should very probably be taking over the transport before long! Riley seemed a bit sick and glum but I didn't see why I shouldn't have it! On Wednesday the Major came up to see me and asked if I really wanted it, or had I asked him in order to straighten out the difficulty of seniority between Riley and myself. I said, that was certainly the primary reason, but on the other hand I thought I should like the job, so he said he would ask the Colonel to give it to me. I wonder how I shall like it – I shall have a lot of draft horses and possibly mules to look after – and a gee to ride myself . . .

Horses were employed by the Army where cars would now be used. Kenneth reported home on a reconnaissance he had to make prior to a field exercise:

> The Captain told me I had better go out to Stretton in the afternoon and make arrangements with the farmer as we are going there for a few days on Monday. So I hired a horse in the town (charging it to the company) and rode out there. I had never ridden in spurs before but I got on quite all right and didn't do any Cossack stunts by the way. I got a good saddle and the horse was quite good except that she kept shying at tree stumps and paper . . . it was about 15 miles but I didn't feel a bit stiff or sore today . . .

The running of such field exercises taught Kenneth to make an administrative plan for the provision of blankets, rations, cooking facilities and transport, tools for entrenching practice, lanterns and officers' kit, and he indented for motor transport in his new-found capacity of transport officer. On arrival at Stretton it was decided that the men could be better employed helping the farmer to grub out a hedgerow and fell some trees, rather than indulge in yet more trench-digging. On 31 January Kenneth described the move to Stretton with wry humour:

> On Monday morning I set to work ordering pounds and pounds of food, hiring a motor lorry and generally arranging the transport for our company who were proceeding to Little Stretton for a week's camping out. By 2.15 I got the lorry loaded up at the Magazine with the camp kitchen, picks and spades, food and men's kit, and we started off, on the way picking up 100 blankets, my camp kit and Simpson's, and we got fairly off and away by about 3 o'clock. The journey was very exciting as we were overloaded and the baggage and everything started shifting to one side – there were three men sitting on the top like monkeys – clinging on by their eyebrows. I roared with laughter, I don't know why but it seemed so funny . . .

With the New Year came a torrent of rumours; orders for the 1st/4th's embarkation, with the rest of the 46th North Midland Division, were expected daily and masses of additional stores were taken on charge by their Quartermaster. On 19 February the entire division received a Royal review by King George V in Great Hallingbury Park, when the massed infantry battalions marched past eight abreast, the Subalterns carrying rifles. Kenneth was still fretting with the reserve battalion, now briefly billeted at Luton prior to assuming the Home Defence role formerly assigned to the 46th Division in the eastern counties. The Orderly Room had been established at 57 Park Street, from where he wrote on 12 February that he was sick in bed with what seems to have been tonsillitis, but had been visited by the CO, Lieutenant Colonel Oliver, and his wife. He also noted that a large new draft of raw recruits had arrived from Billericay, apparently throw-outs from the newly-formed Kitchener Battalion at Leicester, to undergo further training:

> . . . a more hopeless set of men you never saw . . . the majority of them have got crime sheets as long as your arm, two are in the local gaol . . . it seems impossible to do anything with them, they turn round and curse their NCOs and I really don't think they would be above cursing their officers, in fact they do quite openly behind their backs. About a dozen of them have deserted and altogether I think we are going to have trouble with them. Fortunately we in 'A' Company have only got about half a dozen of them but 'D' have got 120! We have got two of our own men at present under lock and key, doing seven days for striking a Corporal – they cut his eye open with a belt buckle . . .

4

OFF TO THE WARS

The appalling casualty rate in France was beginning to tell on the heavily overstretched War Office manning organisation. The old Regular Army had virtually vanished following the attrition of the early battles at Mons, on the River Marne and the First Battle of Ypres. Meanwhile, in the 1st/4th Leicesters now at Bishops Stortford, there was a feeling that embarkation for France was imminent and all ranks were impatient to put their training into practice. Kenneth finally heard, to his undisguised joy, that he was to leave the 2nd/4th, designated as a reserve unit with an unglamorous Home Defence role, for the 1st/4th and the exciting prospect of active service. This was on 19 February, the same day that had seen them paraded for the King, and he sent a scrawled note to his parents: '. . . I am probably off to France next week so I am running down home tomorrow or Sunday to see you. Cheerio – isn't it grand?' His next letter came from Bishops Stortford on the 22nd – a short farewell to the family. Rumour was rife, and Kenneth wrote again on the 24th to allay their fears:

> . . . I was chatting with an Army chaplain, home on a few hours' leave and he seems to think we are going to Havre. Here someone told me that we were probably going to have a 30 hours' sea voyage, so if you should not hear from me for a while, don't get anxious, of course I can't write every day, but I will write to you whenever I get the chance, i.e. at least once a week – above all don't get 'post anxious'. Dear old people . . . well goodnight, God bless you all . . . If I underline the date of my

letter it means send me a roll of No. 1 Brownie film, I think they cost 7d . . .

Kenneth now began to record his service life, and that of his new unit, in considerable detail. During his active service at the Front there is no sign of censorship; he mentions place names and records incidents with a freedom denied him later in the war. Once in France he would be able to send home such trophies as German brass shell cases 'for use as gongs'. Things were now moving fast; morale was high, except among those men who had just got married, many of whom went absent without leave to bid their brides farewell. For all too many this would be a final parting. Kenneth's last letter from Bishops Stortford was written on 26 February. The Officers' Mess, he reported, was in the vestry of a Methodist chapel and the Orderly Room in the offices of Benskins' Brewery. The battalion entrained a day later and the next letter is from Flowers Hotel in Southampton where Kenneth remained for three days, the troops billeted in schools and farmhouses. Goatskin jackets were issued. In the words of the unit historian: 'They were wonderful coats, all sorts of colours, and all smelling strongly of goat, but the men loved them and sounds of "Baa Baa" were heard all over the camp'. There was also an issue of thick socks, '. . . donated by Queen Alexandra and the Women of the Empire'.

The unit sailed for France on 2 March aboard the Thames pleasure steamer *Golden Eagle* (on which Kenneth noted the lamentable catering arrangements) and soon arrived at Le Havre, marching through the town to a tented transit camp where it joined the other battalions of the Leicester and Lincolnshire Brigade in the North Midland Division. Although a number of individual Territorial battalions had been sent to France before Christmas 1914 the 46th North Midland was the first complete Territorial division to go to the Front.

All was novel, especially for men who had probably never left their home county, with the sight of French troops and the sound of a totally foreign language. Messing and sanitary arrangements for all ranks were primitive but, as Kenneth notes, everyone was happy to be there at last. With several fellow officers he was able to walk around the town for an hour or so, enjoying the novelty of their first day in France:

> ... the tram conductors here are mostly women, on account of the shortage of men I suppose. They wear hats like the men and look very smart ... We passed a regiment of French soldiers, in blue overcoats – they looked very business-like ... I must describe the Officers' Mess to you. We each take our mess tins, cups and folding knife, fork and spoon. The Mess is in a large tent ... down the centre is a large trestle table. We sit on forms [benches], or if late on an empty box ... we get our tin full of boiled bully beef, or whatever is going, if it is cold meat it is passed around and we cut off what we want and break off huge pieces of bread. We have been getting bottles of white wine to drink ... For different courses we just wipe our mess tins round with a piece of bread, or use the lid. At night we stick candles down the centre of the table. It is primitive in the extreme but what does it matter, we are all very happy ...

On the evening of 5 March the battalion marched to the railway station to board the train for the Front. Very early the next morning it began its journey, all ranks highly excited by the prospect ahead.

A few days later Kenneth wrote home to describe the journey. Four officers shared a compartment but the men were packed, 38 at a time, into horse wagons. This did not affect their morale and everyone was singing cheerfully as the train moved off. Supplies of bully beef, biscuits, jam, condensed milk and tea had been issued to each wagon and there were periodic halts *en route* enabling the troops to brew up. After 18 hours of spasmodic progress the train pulled up at Cassel, close to the Belgian border, where a confused search for billets was made in the dark; nobody seemed to mind the confusion. Next morning the entire battalion paraded for a church service before marching to the small town of Zuytpeen where new billets were found in farms and factory buildings. Early on the 9th the forward movement continued and late that evening after another rail journey the battalion detrained at Banenchone from where it marched to Strazeele; on the way, General Sir Horace Smith-Dorrien, Commander of the British 2nd Army, was seen standing by the roadside, eyeing the unit professionally and receiving customary compliments from each rifle company as it marched past. At last the unit was within sound of the guns. Kenneth's platoon was lodged in a farm where he shared a room in the farmhouse with two Captains. The troops were accommodated in barns; for the townsmen comprising the majority in the battalion this came as something of a cultural shock, as did the primitive sanitary arrangements to be found on any Flemish farm.

Kenneth quickly acquainted himself with a new set of fellow officers, the soldiers of his platoon, and the key Warrant Officers and NCOs on whom much depended. In later years he was to write an affectionate memoir on his Company Sergeant Major, Warrant Officer Class 2 Bromley, a veteran territorial:

> Straight and true, his life had been one of stern duty. His father died when he was 8 years old, leaving his mother with several young children to bring up. At this early age, Bromley was taken from school and went to work, and when his mother died he still looked after his brothers and sisters and provided them with a home, but he never married . . . Everyone respected him. He went over the top with the 4th Battalion on 13 October 1915 in the attack on the Hohenzollern redoubt. Eight hundred went over, all the officers became casualties, and 188 NCOs and men were left, but their objective was taken. Bromley got a bullet in his thigh. He never went out again but soldiered with the reserve till the end of the war, when he returned to his trade as a 'clicker' [a foreman in Leicester's key shoe industry, responsible for handing out supplies of leather to the bench workers].

As the 17th Regiment of Foot, the Leicesters had marched with Marlborough in these parts 200 years earlier and little had changed as far as billets were concerned; Flemish farms provided cover from the rain and their outbuildings served as troop accommodation, ranged as they were around a courtyard with its steaming midden onto which was thrown every form of garbage as well as the discarded fouled straw from the sheds in which the animals – cows, horses and pigs – were stabled. A slurry pit awaited the unwary and the careless townsman could find himself immersed in this malodorous pond. Chickens wandered around the yard searching for food and a huge dog usually acted as security guard. The barns housing the troops were furnished with straw, on which they slept. The officers, billeted in the farmhouse, were marginally more comfortable, especially if they were able to establish good relations with the farmer and his family. Kenneth, with his professional architect's eye and draughtsman's skill, delighted in drawing the farm buildings in which he and his men were billeted. (Ninety years later it was relatively easy to track some of these billets down and to present the present-day farmer and his family – the third generation to work their farm since 1915 – with photocopies of Kenneth's sketches.)

Training continued, albeit unimaginatively; where the ground permitted, trenches were dug, filled in again, then re-dug, generally in steady rain. Morale suffered, for all ranks were eager to get into the line and put their new-found skills into practice. Kenneth was learning the art of man-management and the need to raise his men's morale as high as possible; they were living in conditions totally alien to townsmen and lacked even basic comforts, for at this stage of the war there were few field canteens where the troops could purchase small luxuries such as soap, cigarettes or confectionery. He wrote home for help:

Can you send me some cigarettes for my men now and then? 'Wild Woodbines' is what they want. Some of the poor chaps haven't had a smoke for days and I think it's a bit rough that they should have to go without here – roughing it like this. I give them what I can myself, as I am all right for baccy, but my store won't last for ever. I am writing to one or two of my friends asking for their cigarettes to give them their little luxury if I possibly can. They are a rough lot of chaps but I think we understand one another and that they appreciate what I try to do for them. I hear one of them remarked one day, 'That's the sort of bloody officer to have'. I had been worrying round for something or other for them . . .

The battalion moved from village to village, ever nearer the Front and Kenneth was as intrigued and appalled as were his men by the ruinous state of countryside that had already been fought over several times in the opening months of the war:

The village has been shelled and there is a row of cottages completely burned out; our transport horses are now stabled there. Nearby is a large factory, one mass of ruins, fallen walls and twisted girders. This afternoon I walked into the next village [Saille sur la Lys] to get some money from the Field Cashier. Quite a number of the houses are pockmarked all over with bullets and shrapnel; the church is completely gutted and used for parking a transport unit with a shoeing forge in one of the chapels.

I did have a game this morning. I bathed my platoon, you would have laughed to have seen them. I borrowed a huge tub from a neighbouring cottage and after filling it with water, put it in the kitchen, and then half the men got into it and washed each other, while the remainder bathed in a stream near by . . .

Kenneth had to undergo a familiar soldier's frustration before long as he was 'left out of battle' when the battalion deployed to the front line near Ploegsteert (known to the troops as 'Plug Street') on a quiet sector as part of its gradual introduction to trench warfare. None of the Leicesters would have dreamt that less than a year

later, Winston Churchill, lately First Lord of the Admiralty but polit-
ically discredited following the failure of the Gallipoli and Dardanelles
expeditions, would be commanding a battalion of the Royal Scots
Fusiliers in the same sector of the line.

On 19 March Kenneth wrote home:

> Woe is me for I am a lonely man. What *do* you think I am
> doing? The whole division has gone off to the trenches and
> here I am in a beastly little farmhouse, in charge of all the sick
> men in the brigade, just because I am the junior Subaltern –
> isn't it just too sickening for words?

The wish of all ranks for real action was about to be fulfilled. Several
moves took place and the battalion had to adjust to new billets. On
the 26th the order finally came and the Leicesters marched out
towards Armentieres '. . . full of curiosity, *esprit de corps* and the joy
of spring' as the battalion's history put it. New billets were found
in a large deserted factory in the suburb of Le Bizet. In this 'quiet'
sector the line was held by two experienced regular battalions, the
1st King's and the 2nd Essex, from whom one company at a time of
the 1st/4th received instruction. Here, it was possible to dig reason-
ably deep trenches and the Leicesters were impressed by those of
their mentors. They learned to their cost that the German snipers
were highly skilled and the first casualties were incurred, usually
through carelessness – unnecessary smoke, a fleeting appearance at
a loophole in the parapet, unguarded movement in view of the
enemy.

It was soon clear that trench warfare involved more boredom,
inactivity and dreary fatigues than fighting. The regulars who had
borne the brunt of the fighting through the autumn of 1914 and
the bitter winter that followed had coined the wry adage that 'The
Germans hold their front with machine guns, the French with field
guns, and the British with men'. A desperate shortage of artillery
ammunition and lack of machine guns compelled the BEF to man
its trenches very much more densely than their foes or allies, and

led to heavy losses from enemy artillery in the first year of the war. While digging a reserve front line the Leicesters soon came under sporadic shellfire. Those of a historical bent noted that a nearby farm bore the date '1702' on its gate, a reminder that their regiment had lived, marched and fought in the same area over two centuries earlier.

The 46th Division remained in reserve, finishing its familiarisation training as the battle of Neuve Chapelle got under way a few miles to the south. This was the first set-piece attack mounted by the BEF since the onset of trench warfare and was entrusted to Haig's 1st Army. The aim was to iron out a salient in the British line and attain the crest of Aubers Ridge from where it was possible to pose a threat to the city of Lille, firmly in German hands. There was to be a fierce preliminary bombardment of the German trench system, for which 100,000 rounds had been allocated. The battle began on the morning of 10 March 1915 in a hurricane of fire lasting only 35 minutes. Initial success was achieved as the German front line was overrun and the salient removed, but the attack lost momentum. The German defensive system based on fields of barbed wire covered by machine guns held up further advance and the battle ended after three days, in which the British suffered over 12,000 casualties. German losses were similar. Some lessons had been learned, but at appalling cost.

In the late autumn of 1914 two opposing armies were facing each other in deadlocked trench warfare which would continue almost to the end of the war. In the opening moves of August the Germans had come close to achieving their aim of capturing Paris by means of a gigantic flanking attack based on the so-called 'Schlieffen Plan'. Devised by the Prussian Field Marshal of that name when Chief of the Great General Staff in the 1890s, it envisaged a drive through Belgium, its left pivoting on the Ardennes with its extreme right flank sweeping round behind Paris, while a decisive battle was to be fought to the east of the capital. All this was a huge gamble, for the General Staff knew that they could be faced with war on two fronts – against the French and British in the west and Imperial

Russia to the east; but they calculated that by the time they had beaten the Allies in the west the Russians, far slower to mobilise, could be tackled in East Prussia. In its original form, Graf von Schlieffen's plan had visualised 'the sleeve of the right hand Prussian grenadier brushing the North Sea' as the advance wheeled through. The concept was however watered down by Schlieffen's successor as Chief of Staff, Helmuth von Moltke, mediocre son of the great soldier who had overwhelmed the French in 1870. The Anglo-French armies managed to halt the Germans on the line of the River Marne east of Paris, then threw them back. Very soon an unbroken trench line stretched from the shores of the North Sea to the Swiss border. On the extreme left of the allied line, along the line of the River Yser, behind an impassable barrier caused by the inundation of large tracts of land, was the small Belgian Army. King Leopold, its nominal commander, established his headquarters near Dixmude on a remaining sliver of Belgian territory. The British and French were able to hold the city of Ypres, creating a salient which would become a huge graveyard for the British Army; this, and the strip of land on the coast held by the Belgian Army was the only piece of unoccupied Belgium and thus of great political importance, even though the city of Ypres was soon no more than a pile of rubble. A few miles to the south lay the tract of country overlooked by the Messines Ridge with which the $1^{st}/4^{th}$ Leicesters would soon be familiar.

5

TRIAL BY FIRE

Following their reverse on the Marne the Germans withdrew to positions on marginally higher ground all along the Front, from which they overlooked the Allies who were forced to dig in on ground which, though barely 50 feet lower than the Messines Ridge line, rapidly became a morass as shellfire demolished the centuries-old Flanders drainage systems. In the late autumn of 1914 unseasonably heavy rains fell, making it impossible to dig adequate trenches on the lower ground. The Germans, on the other hand, were able to create well-drained defensive works, including deep, dry dugouts in the chalk downs where they were firmly ensconced behind ever-thickening fields of wire. The British were compelled to construct sandbag breastworks, as the water table lay only inches below the surface. It was impossible in much of the British sector of the line to construct fieldworks of the sort that Kenneth had so painstakingly drawn and optimistically practised with his men back in Leicester. The best that could be attempted were shallow communication trenches connecting the breastworks, and scooped-out pits further forward in No Man's Land where listening patrols could lurk during the hours of darkness within yards of the German outposts.

The battle of Neuve Chapelle was the first attempt by Sir John French, commanding the BEF, to unlock the stalemate using a headlong infantry assault following a supposedly overwhelming artillery bombardment. There were to be many more such costly attacks, each larger in scale than its predecessors.

So far, Kenneth, as the junior Subaltern in his company, had been unable to satisfy his curiosity about life in the forward trenches;

instead, he had to be content with life as a 'first reinforcement' – in the rear with the assorted sick and temporarily unemployable elements of the brigade. He occupied his spare time by hiring a bicycle (for fourpence an hour) and exploring the local area; on 30 March 1915 he went to Bailleul, the nearest town of any size:

> The roads are wretched round here, if they are not paved they are patched with rough metalling . . . I arrived there without mishap, it is a fairly large town and does not appear to have seen any fighting, but the inhabitants tell me that when the Germans were there they forced the women and children to stand in front of them as a barrier when the English advanced. The place is full of troops and the market place is full of transport and ammunition wagons . . .

Interior of a farm kitchen at Steenwerck, near Bailleul. Kenneth Dalgliesh's training as an architectural draughtsman is evident in all the sketches he made in France and Egypt, and this one is a minor document of social history, depicting a rural way of life long vanished – in this case the farmer is watching over huge pans of cream destined to make cheese.

Farmyard at Le Froid Nid. An officer stands in front of the farmhouse whilst chickens feed off the central midden characteristic of all peasant farms.

On the following day he managed to obtain a lift in a lorry to visit his friends in the battalion, now billeted nearby in the village of Steenwerck. He found the Leicesters in high spirits following their initiation at the front:

> I called at Company HQ to collect my letters. I saw my platoon and they danced around me like a lot of dogs and wanted to know if I was going to take them into the trenches that night. I wish I could have gone back with them but had to come back to look after the beastly sick. I hear they all behaved splendidly under fire and what is more they had one of the hottest corners. Bless 'em. I knew they would be good boys . . .

Whilst they had seen no serious fighting and sustained few casualties they felt, naively as it turned out, that they were proper soldiers now, with something to write home about, and ready to hold their sector of the line. They did not have long to wait. On 1 April their brigade commander told them that they would be sent forward in two or three days' time. The move took place on the 3rd with a march to Dranoutre which took the battalion through Bailleul and into new billets, in farms bearing names such as 'Hyderabad', 'Ava', and 'Kandahar', proclaiming the earlier presence of British units whose service had embraced campaigns in India and Afghanistan. The battalion historian noted that a new commanding officer, Lieutenant Colonel T.T. Greeson of the York and Lancaster Regiment, had taken over from Lieutenant Colonel Harrison, the former territorial CO, recently invalided home, optimistically adding that '. . . now everything would be well with the battalion, a Regular was at the helm . . .'. In the event this proved unfounded for Greeson turned out to be a martinet obsessed with petty detail, given to explosions of wrath if he was not paid the appropriate military compliments. On the eve of Easter he ordered the company commanders forward to reconnoitre their front line positions, which they were to take over from the 1st Monmouths next day; the position lay at One Tree Farm, forward of the villages of Dranoutre and Lindenhoek. The front line lay on the gentle westward slopes of Messines Ridge, overlooked by a ruined building called Spanbroekenmoelen. There was chaos and confusion as the battalion moved forward through waterlogged communication trenches. The distance between the opposing front lines varied from 30 to 100 yards. The intervening ground presented a discouraging spectacle, being covered with the rotting corpses of the 1st Wiltshires and 3rd Worcesters, mown down while carrying out a futile diversionary attack on 12 March during the battle of Neuve Chapelle; a sobering sight for the inexperienced Leicesters.

A week later Kenneth's wait for action was over as he wrote home from the Front on 6 April, reassuring his parents:

> I am in the trenches at last and my word it is a game, you never saw a dirtier or jollier party. We came in here on Sunday night and are in a line of reserve trenches, with little bivvies

and dugouts all along. The one I am in is about 15' by 8' with boarded floor and thick straw (which has never been threshed yet!) . . . Now you dear old parents, don't go worrying yourselves . . . it's just like a picnic from morning till night . . .

He delighted in his men's humorous approach to active service despite the constant shellfire. Conditions in the forward area, however, were extremely uncomfortable owing to the low-lying ground and lack of drainage:

Yesterday it rained all day long and we were kept busy from 4.30 a.m. till 11.30 p.m. draining and repairing the trenches. The wet and mud is really beyond description. I fortunately brought my gumboots with me and have been more than thankful for them. We walk about in anything from 6" to 2' of water and of course clothes get plastered with mud as well . . . the trenches need constant watching especially these dugouts or they would cave in . . . we are some way from the firing trench and so are not exposed to rifle fire, the only thing we get is the stray bullets which patter round about, but they wouldn't hurt you if they hit you. I had them all round me last night when I was working but we were much too busy to take any notice of them . . . it's quite impossible to wash or get undressed and I haven't the slightest wish to attempt either . . . it's funny how quiet the rifles are during the day, hardly a shot is fired, but at night they go at it hammer and tongs, the star shells keep going up one after the other, lighting everything up as clear as day.

The Germans don't know where these trenches are, otherwise we should have been shelled out long ago – however, they have been trying to find our artillery, I have just been outside to watch the shells bursting, but they are very wide of the mark! They come whirring overhead, and make such a funny row, you can actually hear them spinning in the air. And above all there's a lark singing away – what a contrast! . . . Gad,

Sketch by Kenneth Dalgliesh showing the interior of a dugout 'below Mount Kemmel'. By the spring of 1915 the Germans had mastered the art of digging deep galleries in the chalkland, whilst those of the British army were primitive in the extreme, as depicted here.

I do like being in the trenches with my men, if I go into the dugout out of the way of rain or aeroplanes they always want to give me the best place to sit – last night when I was working in the rain and the sludge I felt tired and that I *must* sit down for a while, so I crawled into one of their 'bungalows' (as they call them) and lay down for a spell. After I'd been lying there for a few minutes they thought I was asleep and one of them carefully put a towel over my face because the water was dripping through onto me. It's little actions like this that show me how I stand with them. One of them had made some extra special soup today, and signalled down the trench to me to have some, so I went along and sampled it – my word it *was* good too. They go to 'bed' at night after a hard day's work cursing everybody and everything and in the morning they come out and laugh at the mud and their wet clothes ... I must run down the trench and get my coat, I wrapped one of my men in it this morning, he was ill when I went around, so I gave him a dose of brandy and he has been asleep all morning ... Best of love, dear old family.

Yrs ever, Ken.

In his next letter home, dated 13 April, he describes flooded communication trenches in which it could take up to six hours to struggle two miles in the dark. The battalion was settling into a routine familiar to all who served on the Western Front. Four days 'at rest' in billets some distance to the rear (but still within enemy artillery range) followed by four days forward, either in the fire trenches or in reserve immediately to their rear, from where nightly work took place; this could be improvements to the forward defences, carrying supplies, defence stores such as coils of barbed wire, and ammunition to the fire trenches. And there was the endless task of draining the communication trenches that provided a measure of protection for troops moving to and from the front line. On 15 April Kenneth described this routine:

I am in the 'dugouts' again behind the firing line, we came here on Monday night and have been working practically day and night ever since and we are all just too utterly tired for words ... I am looked upon as somewhat of an authority on rebuilding dugouts!! We get an awful lot of shelling here and quite enjoy the sport, we have never been actually shelled ourselves (as we are a secret) but on Tuesday I was walking down the trench and watched a farmhouse about 700 yards away being shelled ... the building was full of Tommies when the fun began; my word, you should have seen them come running out, they didn't stop to put on their hats and coats ...

During the night we do entirely different work, we go up to battalion headquarters and act as fatigue parties, carrying

A front line trench on the lower slopes of Messines Ridge, April 1915, as seen from Kenneth Dalgliesh's dugout entrance. Note the trench sentry's position, looking out obliquely to the front in order to avoid sniping. Also the officer's revolver on a sandbag, ready for instant use, the brazier at the entrance, and the rum jar at the sentry's feet.

rations, water, fuel, ammunition, sandbags, etc. up to the firing trenches. It's really quite good fun if one wasn't so dog tired – I usually enjoy the first trip but if one is sent up a second time it's no joke.

Daylight revealed scenes of unimaginable devastation. Ahead lay the gentle but commanding slopes of Messines Ridge on which the Germans were deeply entrenched behind fields of barbed wire, their forward outposts less than 50 yards uphill from the Leicesters' own listening posts. From there they commanded a clear view over the British trenches downhill and well to the rear towards Bailleul. To the north, German observers could see the higher ground around Kemmel Hill which would remain in British hands until taken in the German offensive of March 1918. By contrast the British forward positions – the so-called fire trenches – were mainly above ground, as digging here was impossible, and at first there was no continuous front line. Supply of drinking and washing water was a great problem and resort had to be made to boiling that which was scooped up from the communication trenches, often dangerously near the reeking latrine pits and the unburied dead. It was undrinkable even when chlorinated and scarcely adequate for ablutions. Rations and drinking water had to be manhandled through knee-deep mud in the waterlogged communication trenches; troops in the very forward positions had little to eat except bully beef and hard biscuit as the lighting of fires for boiling up tea drew immediate enemy fire. All ranks in the actual firing line were wet, cold, exhausted and miserable in such conditions. The stench of decay, mingled with that of human excrement, was all-pervasive despite lavish use of powdered chloride of lime as disinfectant. French troops previously holding this sector had ignored even the basics of field sanitation, leaving their positions in a filthy condition, with numerous unburied dead. The strain of nightly fatigues soon made itself felt and Kenneth had to use all his powers of persuasion to keep the men at their arduous and dangerous work:

Front line trenches of the 1st/4th Leicesters below Messines Ridge. This is Kenneth Dalgliesh's sketch of the same stretch of trench shown in the following press photograph, but shows it as it was immediately after construction (or repair). Due to the high water table it was impossible to dig deeper than about three feet and the British front line at this point relied on 'Sangars' – barriers of sandbags above ground level – in order to obtain a measure of protection for those manning the forward positions. German shellfire wrecked these and they had to be repaired nightly, a duty allocated to KD for much of his time at the front.

BREAKING NEWS

TRIBUTE: MUSEUM PLANS TO RECREATE TRENCH IN MEMORY OF TROOPS

Revisiting horror of war

BY CHRISSY HARRIS

It is the place where many of Leicestershire's war heroes fought and died.

Now, this muddy trench dug into a Belgian field is to be re-created in a new museum dedicated to the soldiers' memory.

Experts are hoping to piece together a replica of Trench 47, in Ypres, Belgium, for an exhibit at the Leicester Tigers Museum, due to open in October 2005.

Visitors will be able to step back to 1915 and gain some sense of the horrific conditions members of the 4th Battalion Leicester Regiment Territorial Force endured during the First World War.

To add to the "Trench Experience", regimental historian Richard Lane is trying to trace relatives of the four soldiers in the black-and-white photo. If successful, his plan is to include their details in the exhibit.

COME ON **THE TIGERS**

He said: "This will give people an idea of what life was like and what our boys went through. It was horrendous.

WHAT HAPPENED TO THEM? Four Leicestershire soldiers at Ypres, 1915 – Pte Foulkes, Cpl Kent, Sgt Burdett and Sgt Gibbons

the people in the photo. We'd   to be able to see what their an-

Four Leicestershire soldiers in the trench at Messines Ridge. (Photo: *Leicester Mercury*)

I went up twice last night – it wasn't that I was so tired myself, but the men had been digging all day and were played out and I had *such* a job to get them along – you see we *must* get back before dawn. We don't go along that flooded trench now, we take practically a bee-line across country over ditches, thro' farmyards, across fields etc. etc., and every time a star-shell goes up we have to lie down or stand stock still until it has gone down, then we move on again. The shell holes are an awful nuisance, we slip into them and scramble out again, oh we do get into such a mess, we are up here for four days and we never wash or shave, and our clothes are plastered with yellow mud – then we go back to our billets and rest for four days . . .

Kenneth saw the impact of war on the peasant farmers who tilled the rich soil of the region; on his way up to the front to repair and drain the trenches, he was shocked by the devastation where the French had recently fought:

On our way forward we passed through a farmyard – all ruins – three dead dogs in one place, the skeleton of a horse, and the decaying carcase of a pig (evidently hit by a shell fragment as he was running out of his sty). We passed through the orchard and by gad they must have fought there and there are no less than four lines of trenches in it, ground won by yards, almost feet. Halfway up the track is another farm, I crept over to have a look at it and never saw such a mass of desolation; practically a heap of bricks, everything burnt that would burn, a crumpled bedstead in one room, the remains of a fireplace in another, and the rotting remains of a man in the passage. Outside are the stinking carcases of pigs and a little further off a group of five horses, slowly rotting away, harness and all, evidently part of a gun team. There is a grave too, where one of the gunners lies, his hat on the small wooden cross, it must have been there for months, but no one would dream of moving it . . . I have told you a lot of horrid things, haven't I? I can see old mother shuddering, bless her, but somehow we never think much of these things. I have seen dozens of dead men, but it seems quite natural now – there's an artillery duel going on over my head at the present moment but I really can't be bothered to go outside and look at it . . .

The battalion was learning its trade under relatively quiet conditions. Kenneth's introduction to the dangers of the firing line came towards the end of April. On the 23rd – St George's Day – he described his first experience of survival in one of the exposed listening posts only yards from the German positions. There were several of these on the battalion's frontage, sited forward of the main trench line – now more or less continuous as orders had been given from on

high to ensure an unbroken line from the Belgians on the left of
the BEF to the French on the right. The posts were reached from
the front line by crawling along shallow trenches. Two of them,
known as 'E2' and 'E3', were recognised as being particularly
dangerous, but 'E1' was even worse:

> Here I am, right bang in the front line of trenches with the
> Germans only about 100 yards off . . . these are quite the best
> trenches I have been in, big sandbag parapets and though it's
> a bit wet, we at least have wooden grids to walk on. My first
> duty when I came in on Tuesday was to take out the listening
> patrol – I wasn't at all looking forward to the job but it wasn't
> half as bad as I expected. I take an NCO and five men and
> we creep out of the corner of the trench and down to three
> listening pits where the men lie until about 3 a.m. to watch
> and listen. I don't stop with them, I come back directly I have
> posted them – poor beggars, they get very cold lying there.
> When this is done, I have working parties on repairing the
> sandbag parapets which the Germans have shot away during
> the day, draining the trenches, and last night re-building my
> 'dugout'. When I have got them all at work I walk round my
> sentries to see they are all awake and I have pot shots up and
> down the line to see if the Germans are awake! Now and then
> I fire a star-shell [actually, a flare from a Verey Pistol] which
> lights up the German lines and my men fairly rattle it into
> them then – I'm getting quite expert at dropping these star
> shells into their trenches. This goes on till 1.30 a.m. with occa-
> sional visits to the listening posts, when I am relieved by Capt
> Haylock . . .

After this, Kenneth was able to crawl into his dugout – in this case
little more than a crude shelter, most of which had to be above
ground level due to the high water table – and snatch an hour's
sleep before rising at 3.30 a.m. when the entire unit in the front line
stood to arms for an hour, the routine 'stand-to' in case of a surprise

attack at dawn when the rising sun would be in the defenders' eyes. This lasted for another hour, after which the day sentries had to be posted and working parties organised. He could then lie down in hope of another hour's rest until breakfast at 8 a.m.:

> Bacon and eggs – my man brought a dozen with him – after which I stroll around inspecting generally, visit the neighbouring trenches and take it as easy as my Captain permits . . . I went for quite a long walk this morning into the neighbouring battalion's trenches and in sight of Ypres – yesterday I had spotted a couple of loopholes with my periscope and was directing a man when to fire when *bang* and my periscope disappeared, the beggars had drilled a bullet clean through the top – it made me jump! . . . It is lovely spring here and there are fields and fields of kingcups and cowslips – I always think of mother when I see kingcups and celandines. The trees, at least those that have not been shattered and drilled by bullets are all bursting out into green – if it wasn't for the noise and stink one could not realise it is war.

Since arriving at the front, Kenneth had been looked after by his soldier-servant or batman, Private Orton, who went everywhere with him as his personal bodyguard and when at rest in billets saw to his washing and other domestic chores. Their relationship grew, based on mutual respect. Kenneth reports in a letter dated 27 April that while returning from the forward positions to their billet with a working party, Orton jumped down into a ditch and sprained his ankle. Kenneth hauled him out, laid him down by the roadside and hurried back to the billets where he found a carrying party to bring the casualty in. His continual concern for the men under his command shows him to have been a dedicated Subaltern, despite his lack of formal training for the job.

The sector on which the Leicesters were serving was becoming more active; the day after Orton's mishap. Kenneth was writing home again:

The trench sentry on the left is Kenneth Dalgliesh's soldier-servant Private Orton, who would behave so admirably when Kenneth was wounded. Further along the trench is Kenneth's platoon sergeant, Sgt Black.

Yesterday at 2 p.m. our artillery started a terrific cannonade north of us [i.e. in the Ypres sector] which has been going on ever since. I think it is to last something like 72 hours but we shall not get a look-in at it. I have never heard anything like it, it is just one continuous rumble of reports tumbling over one another. When you think what a shell costs you can have a small idea of what a war costs. It is really a fine sunny day but the sky even here is thick with yellow smoke from the guns, like a London fog.

By the way, the Germans have started using gas, the dirty dogs! We did not get it very badly in our trench but the neighbouring battalion had to put wet cloths over their mouths and noses; it simply made our eyes smart . . .

The Germans were the first to use gas on the Western Front, releasing clouds of it on 22 April to launch the Second Battle of Ypres. They had already tried it out against the Russians on the Eastern Front earlier in the year, using a form of tear gas with little apparent success. On this occasion, at Ypres, a far more lethal gas was used. Based on chlorine it attacked the respiratory tract and flooded men's lungs, virtually drowning them if they lacked any protection. In the initial attack at Langemarck, north-east of Ypres, a cloud of chlorine was released without warning against two French divisions whose mainly colonial African troops broke and fled, streaming *en masse* to the rear, spreading panic as they ran. The neighbouring Canadian division held its ground, to be subjected to a second gas attack a few days later. By then, improvised gasmasks, in the form of cloths soaked in chemicals (and as a last resort, urine) had been made available and the line held.

Had he but known it, Kenneth's service on the Western Front was almost at an end. After a hard day's work on trench fatigues he had returned to his dugout at 7 p.m. on 29 April when orders came from the Adjutant for him to report to battalion headquarters. As it was already dark he did not use the flooded communication trench and made his way forward, with the faithful Orton at his side, simply by walking across open ground. On arriving safely he was told to go further forward with a working party of 20 men to repair part of the forward trench system and improve the listening posts. Kenneth and his party moved cautiously forward up a new communication trench and worked hard all night. While the soldiers continued with repairs to the battered defences, Kenneth was seeing to the listening posts, even further forward and only yards from the Germans:

> I wanted to take them further out. I started off with the one on the left and took a couple of sappers out with me as well, as they knew more about the lie of the ground than anyone, and moreover they seemed to have an idea of the positions of the German listening post; they told me they had seen them one night within 15 yards of our parapet. We got out of the trench and crawled over a lot of rough ground, shell holes and all the usual trench muck, then through a line of old French barbed wire, past a post and rail fence and then a little way along to the left. I lay there a long time and discussed the ground with the sappers and then returned the way I had come and visited my patrol on the right. I was not at all satisfied with their position – not nearly far enough out – so I spent practically the remainder of the night crawling about over the mass of disused trenches between the outposts. They were filthy, half full of soft mud, so that I was obliged to do most of my crawling on the top . . . Once during the night I came up to my patrol on the further side and gave them a bit of a fright – they weren't expecting anyone; however, there wasn't any risk of their shooting me – listening patrols don't use their rifles, bayonets are much quieter!

After the 'stand-to' at dawn I lay down for a few hours' sleep, breakfasting between 8 and 8.30. It's strange what a keen nose the Hun has for fried bacon; whenever we started to fry he'd set to work and snick the top of our parapet, sending a cloud of sand and grit over the frying pan. I suppose it pleased him to hear the good English that followed! Breakfast over, I started down the communication trench to visit the neighbouring outpost but had not gone a dozen yards before a man came running after me to say one of my men was hit. It was a case of sniping; we had been trying to locate the fellow earlier in the morning. I did not stop to see the poor chap then but ran round as fast as I could to see if I could get a bomb thrown at the spot where I thought the sniper lay. I had never seen a man in my charge hit before and it made me wild. I then returned to see what I could do for him, but I could see at a glance that he was beyond all human aid – his brains were in his hat, the bullet had gone through his head and there he lay, poor fellow, just sobbing his life away. Some of the others suggested bringing him in, but I wouldn't have him disturbed, and I lay under a waterproof sheet with him while he died. He never spoke, he was unconscious from the moment he was hit.

Kenneth and his men were now as close to the enemy as it was possible to get, under horrifying conditions in a sector of the Front that had seen much action and was littered with hundreds of the unburied dead – British, French and German. Even in the support trenches, where officers and men sought as much rest as they could, life was perilous, for the German shellfire was heavy, claiming many casualties from those rash enough to remain in the open.

Life in the listening posts was unpleasant but junior officers had to take their turn of duty there. The official war diary of the 4th Leicesters describes them vividly:

E1. This trench is in two parts, E1 Left and E1 Right. Separated by 30–40 yards of old trench . . . Exposed position and liable to enfilade fire and sudden assault, but very important . . . men should only be in this trench 24 hours and then relieved. Ground all round is unsanitary.

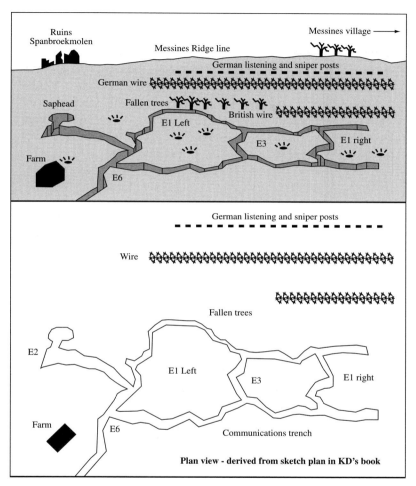

Plan view - derived from sketch plan in KD's book

This rough sketch depicts the trench layout at the point where KD was wounded. *Above* – a notional oblique view, and *below*, the vertical trench map. The Leicesters' trenches were halfway up a gentle slope leading to the summit of Messines Ridge. The village of Messines itself lies about 400 yards to the right of this sketch and the main German trenches, with their deep dugouts in the chalk, lie along the ridge line, with their listening posts about 200 metres forwards on the slope, overlooking the British positions. The Leicesters' listening posts, E1 Left and E1 Right, were regarded as by far the most dangerous places to be and KD was wounded when trying to negotiate a fallen tree between the two.

The battalion historian enlarges on the situation at E1 Left:

> It would take more than the pen of Edgar Allen Poe to describe truthfully the gruesomeness, the noisome atmosphere, and the unutterable filth of E1 Left. The Regulars had called it 'Hell's Kitchen' . . . it consisted of an isolated sandbag barricade . . . built on dead bodies of both French and British which had been partially smothered with filth and chloride of lime; it was about 15 yards in length and 30 yards from the German lines, and slightly below them. It had no shelter of any sort when the Leicesters arrived though afterwards it was improved slightly and a dugout built. It deployed listening patrols of two men each to its right and left fronts and the occupants sent up flares most of the night . . .

After losing one of his men to a sniper, Kenneth continued to work on the repair of the badly damaged defences in the front line:

> The rest of the day was taken up with the writing of reports, indenting for materials etc., and perhaps 40 winks. I was relieved in the evening just after dusk and went down to SP2A, a supporting post in the rear where I was relieved by Lt Forsell. SP2A is a quiet place; after I had been round the trench, seen that the sentries were posted and said 'how do' to the machine gun Sergeant, I crept into my dugout and lay down on a pile of nice clean straw and slept all night (with my feet out of the door so that the sentry could kick me if necessary). The next day was uneventful until about 2.30 when I was inspecting the machine gun – the Sergeant was explaining the mechanism to me when the Huns started to shell us. We all bolted into our dugouts like rabbits but the Sergeant wouldn't come in until he had taken his gun off its tripod and brought it under cover – he loves it like a child – he wasn't going to have it knocked about by any bally Germans, no not he, he'd got a lot of work for that little chap to do!

The final 24 hours of Kenneth's service at the Front are vividly described in his own words. It was near E1, while searching for the site of a new post, that his active service came to an abrupt halt. In the terse words of the battalion's historian: 'Second Lieut K. Dalgliesh sups off toasted cheese, goes out to visit the listening posts, gets a bullet in the arm and carries an empty sleeve for the rest of his life'.

Following his visit to the machine gun Sergeant and the German barrage from which they both had to seek cover, Kenneth continues:

After the Germans had had their whack our artillery set to work and plumped them over in fine style, we were able to come out of our dugouts then, and wished them luck as they went spinning over our heads when suddenly I heard one coming up that seemed like a lame dog compared to the others. I was just remarking on it to the machine gun Sergeant when it dropped in a ruined farm behind us – fortunately it did not explode. I was determined to have a look at it, so after dark I went out with one of my men to locate it. We hadn't gone far when I picked up the brass nose-cap and, a little further off, was the shell, unexploded.

I returned to the trench soon after and had a telephone call from the Adjutant, who instructed me to return to E1 Left. I assure you that I said a few polite words to myself; I was very comfortable where I was; however, 'orders is orders' as the men say, so I collected a certain number of men together and started off. It was a rotten bit of ground that we had to cross to get up to the firing line, almost on a level with the German lines, and the bullets whistled unpleasantly near to our heads, so that every now and then we had to lie down. Well, I got to E1 Left without mishap and relieved the little garrison there. As before, the night was taken up with repairing the parapet, it was in a worse state than usual and I was obliged to keep all my men, with the exception of the sentries and listening patrols, hard at work carrying sandbags while a corporal and I built the parapet.

Once more during the night I went out and explored the ground again between us and the next advance post on the right to endeavour to find a more suitable position for my listening patrol on this side. While out, I ran up against a party of engineers and told the Sergeant in charge what I was trying to find. He at once said he knew the very place I wanted and very kindly came along to show me. He took me up to the back of my patrol and we rolled over the fallen tree trunk they were lying behind and crawled forward until we were under the branches of another tree that was lying towards us. It was a much better position and I could see right in front of my own parapet and also had a splendid view of the German parapet which was only 30 yards away at this point. I lay there and examined the ground in front of me, while the Sergeant went back and fetched the rest of my patrol up. He warned us not to go too far to our left as there was a dead man there – we went up to have a look at him but he was too far gone to be recognisable, he was lying in a shell hole half full of water and quite impossible to bury. After this I returned to my advance post and resumed the repairing of the parapet in places to protect us from the enfilading fire to which the Huns treated us on both sides.

About half an hour before dawn my listening patrol on the left came in as they said they had been fired on. I promised them a good dressing down later for having come in before time. But it set me thinking about my patrol on the right in the new and more advanced position I had chosen. It was getting near dawn (3.30) and they hadn't returned, and I began to get uneasy and imagine things – perhaps one of them had been hit and the other couldn't get him in, so off I went.

I got up to the first fallen tree all right and cautiously looked over, but I couldn't see them. I called very quietly to them but couldn't see or hear anything, so I proceeded to roll over the tree trunk, but had not got my leg over before there was a sharp crack and I found myself lying in a heap with an indescribable something in my arm and knee. I never can describe what it felt like but there was no mistaking that I had 'stopped one'. I had so often read of men being 'wounded', 'casualty lists of wounded', and now I thought to myself 'I am wounded'. All these thoughts and many more came crowding into my head as I lay there.

I looked down at my left arm and saw that it was all ribbons and the blood was flowing pretty freely, and realised that I must get back to my advanced post before I got too weak to move, so I tried my arm and finding I could bend it, I crawled a little way, but fearing that I might 'black out' I got up and ran the remaining distance, certainly my record sprint!

When I got to the advance post I told them to send for a 'dresser' at once as I had been hit in the arm and knee, and then sat down on a pile of sandbags. My Sergeant immediately cut my sleeve away and got hold of my arm and tried to find the arteries to stop the flow of blood; he hung onto it like grim death until his thumbs were numbed. I naturally began to feel a bit weak and bethought myself of the flask of brandy I carried in my breast pocket, but not a drop was there, the bullet had blown the flask to pieces and had then been turned a little to one side by the nickel mirror and pocket book which I carried in the same pocket, after which it entered my arm and ripped it open almost from one end to the other. The mirror and pocket book had undoubtedly saved my life.

Had the bullet not been parried
By the brandy flask I carried,
Mine had been an early grave.
Ne'er had heart so close a shave.

A Royal Army Medical Corps dresser was soon on the scene. He fixed a tourniquet and Kenneth was expertly bandaged. As it was impossible for stretcher-bearers to get along the front trenches the only way to get to the rear was by walking along narrow communication trenches to the regimental aid post where the battalion medical officer could carry out further immediate treatment. Leaving his Sergeant in command of the advance post, Kenneth, escorted by two soldiers, started back along the trench system to a fellow officer's dugout where he lay down; his wounds were stiffening and he was now in great pain, as much from his tourniquet as from the actual wounds. Here he was found by the Medical Officer who treated him on the firing step as it was too dark in the dugout; he was still worried about his men in the listening post and no one could reassure him that they had got back safely (he was relieved to be told, much later, that they were safe). Although the wounded were seldom moved to the rear in daylight because of the risk of detection by enemy observers who would then be able to pinpoint the layout of the communication trenches, permission was given for Kenneth to be stretchered back to where he could be transferred to an ambulance and evacuated to a field hospital. The journey back through the trench systems seemed endless and at times Kenneth had to dismount from his stretcher and make his own way, sometimes crawling to avoid detection from the German lines; he was now feeling sleepy and was grateful when a gunner officer offered him a drink as he passed back through the gun lines:

> It seemed as if we would never get out of the trenches, sometimes the corners were so sharp that the stretcher bearers had to lift me up on a level with the parapet and I expected every minute to get another bullet; however, we eventually got out into the road and passed along the back of the artillery lines . . . things were very quiet then, and the gunners were standing about in groups, smoking. An officer came up and asked me if I was badly hit and whether he could get me anything. I told him I'd love a cup of tea so he tore off down the road to an Estaminet where the ambulance was waiting. He wasn't able to get any tea but brought me a glass of milk. I often think of him and his kindness, for we didn't know one another from Adam, and I wish him luck.

6

RECOVERY

Kenneth was taken by ambulance to a casualty clearing station at Bailleul where his wounds received further treatment. His soldier-servant, Private Orton, followed him for six miles down from the line on foot:

> I was fortunate in not losing any of my kit, and it was entirely due to my servant. He collected the stuff I had in the trench with me, and walked all the way to Bailleul, calling on the way for my valise which was at the close billets. This, together with his own pack and rifle was no light load. He came to see me on the Sunday and also on the Monday morning, and tho' I asked him several times to get my purse out of my trousers so that I might pay him his week's wage [it was the custom for officers to augment their soldier-servant's meagre pay out of their own pocket to compensate them for their extra duties] – he would not do so.

In a memoir privately written for his family many years later Kenneth recalled the devotion of Private Orton:

> . . . who collected all my possessions and carried them on his shoulders, plus his rifle, to the hospital in Bailleul where I had been taken. He stowed them under my cot, said 'goodbye' and went into the courtyard where the Sister found him crying his heart out. Poor rough, faithful Orton, he got his right elbow smashed with a bullet a week afterwards.

The two men maintained contact, writing to each other as they recovered from their wounds. Kenneth stayed only two days at Bailleul before his further evacuation to a military hospital at Boulogne where the surgeons amputated his left arm. By now his parents had received a letter, dated 2 May, from the devoted nursing Sister at the Bailleul clearing station:

Dear Mr and Mrs Dalgliesh,

I wish to say that your son, Lt Dalgliesh, has been brought in here *very* seriously wounded in the shoulder. Everything possible is being done for him by the surgeons and nurses here. I let you know at once as I know how anxious you will be at hearing from the War Office. We are *very very* busy as you can imagine. I will write again in a day or two. Your son is very anxious that you do not worry about him, he says I am to tell you he is all right. I hope to give you a good account next time I write – believe me,

Yrs truly, Kathleen Matthews, Sister in Charge.

Kenneth was able to scrawl a pencilled note home to reassure his parents when obviously still in shock and pain:

Dear old people,

I have sent you a field post card but they seem to read all wrong when you get to the base so I'll try and drop you a line but I can't every day. I had your dear letter yesterday . . . The doctor says he thinks they'll ship me over some time this week, so I shouldn't worry about passport if they are making a lot of fuss. I am going on splendidly,

Best of love to you all. God bless you all, Ken.

A telegram followed on the 4th, as Kenneth was clearly desperate to spare his parents any worry: 'In hospital 7th Stationary, Boulogne. Wounded left arm. Amputation probable. Otherwise doing well.' It was followed within hours by a postcard, despatched before the cable but aimed at maintaining his parents' morale: 'Monday: I have flesh wound in the left forearm and am at Boulogne. I shall be here for a few days . . . love to all.' The correspondence comes to a temporary halt at this point, although it is clear that he did in fact keep up his letter writing, both to friends and family and to Orton. Early in June, while convalescing in England, Kenneth received a postcard from the Reverend Mac Liebenrood, an Army chaplain based at Folkestone: 'Your soldier servant Private Orton is in hospital here wounded through the right arm and doing well. He seemed devoted to you and so I promised to write and try and find you out . . .'

Orton had not been seriously wounded and was able to write his own account in a letter which Kenneth received a few days later. It is a remarkable document, not only as a testament to a soldier-servant's loyalty to his officer but also as evidence of the literacy of a generation of men who received little or no education past the age of 13 or 14 but were taught rigorously in their elementary schools what were then known as 'the three Rs' – reading, writing and arithmetic – and could write legibly, although this one was laboriously penned shakily by Orton's left hand and later transcribed by Kenneth. It is quoted in full as it provides a rare insight into the life and attitude of a private soldier on the Western Front.

June 7th 1915
My dear Sir,

I was very pleased to hear from you the other day as I have been wondering how you are getting on, as I have not heard any news of you since I left the hospital you were in at France. I am very sorry indeed that that you have had to lose your arm and hope that you will soon be strong again. I shall never forget that day in the trenches and how plucky you were after being wounded and I am sure the officers and men of the company were all proud of you because you did not only think of yourself but of others who were on that listening patrol and I am sure that your platoon were lost without you and were wondering who we were going to have to keep the roughs together as you know they were rough but their hearts were in the right place. I shall never forget when I left you in the hospital, when I got outside I had to have a good cry as I was full up. When I got to the billets that morning the boys had just come out and altho' they were about beat, they hung around me enquiring how you were getting on, and every one of those men got in, those who you went to get in.

All went on as usual out of the trenches, inspections as usual, then we marched off again. I was posted to Mr —'s platoon to do servant, as his servant went sick, me being lucky had to go into the 'butcher's shop'. The first day we had M— killed and I was wounded myself. I had one through the right forearm, the bullet breaking both bones. I have lost use of my hand but the doctor has told me I shall get that back again in time. Corporal R— Pte G— and poor Cpl X— all got done in the same place. E1 Left. Dear Sir, I hope you got hold of all your kit as I was worrying about that. I will now close as it is hard work writing with my left hand.

Your obedient servant, Pte Orton.

A delighted Kenneth was thus enabled to regain touch with the faithful Orton and their friendship endured thereafter; Orton's wound prevented him, as well as his master, from returning to the Front. Indeed, Kenneth's severe wound probably saved his life, for of the 29 officers of the $1^{st}/4^{th}$ Leicesters who served with the battalion in France and Flanders before April 1915, 12 had been killed in action or died of wounds by the end of the year. He continued to correspond with Orton, and was able to send him the balance of his batman's extra-duty pay, which was promptly acknowledged:

Manor House Hospital
Folkestone
(undated)

Dear Sir,

I was v. pleased to hear from you again and also to hear you are
getting along as well as can be expected. I have not had any news
from the Front for some time now so I am sorry I cannot let
you know how the boys are getting on. You wrote and ask(ed)
me about poor Mr Waite [killed in action 7 June 1915]; I saw his
name in the paper a few weeks ago and I am very sorry for our
Captain Fielding Johnson [wounded] there was a gentleman came
to this hospital visiting and he told me he had come from the
Leicesters and had read [of] our Captain being killed. My arm is
getting along but they thought I had got to have another operation but I had to go under the X-ray and the doctor told me it
was doing well. Dear Sir, you wrote to ask me if I knew where
to go when I am discharged from hospital all I know is to go
and report at the Magisene (*sic*) Leicester and then I expect I will
be sent to another batt, I think I will now close thanking you
very much for the Postal Order hoping to see you again soon
and make haste and gain some more weight.

I remain yours truly, Orton.

The supreme test of the 1ˢᵗ/4ᵗʰ Leicesters was to come in October
1915. After Kenneth's departure the battalion continued to occupy
positions below the Messines Ridge, then later in the summer at
Sanctuary Wood and Hill 60, two spots in the Ypres salient that
would acquire ominous significance later in the war but were still
relatively quiet at this stage. Even so, their historian records that the
Adjutant and Medical Officer were killed at this time by shellfire
outside their dugout in the comparative safety of a supposedly safe
'rest' area on the outskirts of Ypres town.

Political considerations, chiefly pressure put upon the British government by the French to increase the military effort in France, led to Kitchener's instruction to a reluctant Field Marshal Sir John French, directing him to support the hard-pressed Allied army and its imminent offensive in Champagne, which was duly launched on 25 September as the BEF attacked in the mining area around Hulloch to the south of Ypres in the first phase of what became known as the Battle of Loos. Haig, commanding the British 1st Army entrusted with the operation, was as unwilling to open an offensive at this stage as his Commander in Chief; he was aware of the limitations of the untried troops under his command and the desperate shortage of artillery ammunition due to shortcomings of the armaments industry at home. Kitchener was insistent, ordering the BEF to do its utmost to help the French in their offensive, even if by doing so it could suffer very heavy losses. Until now, Sir John French had managed to resist his allies' insistent demands to attack and had told the French leaders, Foch and Joffre, that the most he could do at this time was to provide some artillery support. His best infantry had already suffered appallingly and the old Regular Army had all but disappeared. Until the Territorial Force had acquired the necessary experience, the New Armies trained and kitted out to an acceptable operational standard, and above all, the artillery provided with adequate supplies of high explosive ammunition and the heavy guns needed to break into the German defences, the British Army could not render the support for which the French clamoured. The political and strategic imperatives for a British offensive were augmented by the need to take pressure off the hard-pressed Russians in the east.

As if problems of manpower and *materiel* were not enough to convince Haig and French that an attack in the autumn of 1915 would invite disaster, losses to the rapidly decreasing pool of Camberley-trained staff officers placed enormous strain on the depleted headquarters at brigade, divisional, corps and army levels, facing the huge workload of operational and logistic planning. Despite this, and knowing that the omens for success were unfavourable,

Haig's staff officers, and those of his two subordinate corps, set about their preparations. As for the troops now committed, in the words of the official history, HQ BEF '. . . knew that their divisions were not yet the instruments demanded by the exigencies of modern war'. Raw, semi-trained, ill equipped and led, thousands of patriotically enthused officers and men were about to be tried in the fire. Zero hour was on 25 September and for the first time the British elected to use gas, released an hour before the infantry assault, in order to compensate for lack of artillery preparation. This was only a partial success as the clouds drifted back onto the British lines in many places. Although the Hohenzollern Redoubt, an enormously strong pivot of the German defences, was taken by the 9th Scottish Division, together with the village of Loos, albeit at great cost, the Germans counter-attacked and regained these objectives. The British reserves had been deployed too far to the rear for their intervention to be effective; and in any case the two inexperienced Kitchener divisions earmarked for exploiting any success achieved by the assaulting formations were held up as they struggled forward through congested communication trenches, then launched, after a chaotic night march, against uncut wire and machine guns with predictable results.

In the initial phase of the battle the 4th Leicesters had been given the role of creating a diversion by igniting straw previously laid in front of their trenches, but after a downpour of rain it was sodden and would not light. This improvised smoke-screen therefore failed. The real trial was yet to come. The battalion was moved further south in the Loos sector early in October for a further attempt to take the Hohenzollern. During a visit from General Allenby, the battalion's CO, Lieutenant Colonel Martin, made it clear that too many inexperienced and under-trained officers and men were being sent out as reinforcements. This availed him little; the training organisation in the United Kingdom had yet to attain the momentum needed to provide a rapidly expanding field army with much-needed junior leaders. It was now clear that the 46th North Midland Division's untried troops were expected to recapture the Hohenzollern Redoubt.

The COs and company commanders of the battalions entrusted with the attack were acquainted with the lie of the land by visits to the forward trenches from where they could examine their fearsome objective through trench periscopes. General Stuart-Wortley was able to confirm the task facing the 4th Leicesters when he told the company commanders that the end of static trench warfare – what he breezily described as '. . . this caddish sort of fighting', was over and that the impending attack signalled the commencement of open warfare with the '. . . joy and glory of going over the top'. The reaction of his audience is not reported, but in the words of their battalion's historian:

> they had become veterans in easy stages . . . had always given a good account of themselves and they were now really coming to close quarters with the enemy and intended to show the soldiers of the Fatherland that King George V as well as King George III had some astonishing infantry that would take some stopping.

Such was the optimistic spirit of the times.

The final days before the main attack were taken up in rehearsal, grenade training, and instruction by the Royal Engineers in the art of reversing the parapets of captured trenches. All officers and most of the NCOs visited the forward trenches to see for themselves the ground over which they would be attacking. The corps commander, Lieutenant General Haking, addressed all the senior officers in the attacking division, assuring them that the preliminary artillery bombardment, augmented by gas, would be on such a scale that little or no opposition could be expected from the defenders of the Hohenzollern Redoubt. He would certainly have known that most of the available gun ammunition was shrapnel – deadly against unprotected troops in the open but useless for cutting the enemy's wire and destroying his fieldworks. Much of the high explosive ammunition now needed for the attack on Hohenzollern had been diverted to the Dardanelles where Hamilton's stranded expedition had encountered similar problems as its troops repeat-edly launched courageous but futile attacks on well-entrenched Turkish positions. On the Western Front the French were planning to use 5,000 guns to ensure an irresistible barrage as they launched their offensive. Haig had asked for no less than 36 divisions to ensure success in his attack; he was given 9, and although his artillery commander had 47 heavy and nearly 900 field pieces at his disposal, such was the parlous ammunition supply that these were restricted to a firing rate of one round per gun every 11 minutes.

The battlefield was in a coal-mining area amidst slag heaps and winding gears of numerous collieries, interspersed with flat open terrain, devoid of cover and thus difficult for the attacking troops. Fresh formations, including the 46th Division, were brought up for a second assault, due on 13 October. Going into the line late on the evening of 12 October the Leicesters were somewhat awed to be relieving a battle-worn battalion of the Guards Division, who had recently repulsed a German attack, inflicting very heavy casu-alties on the enemy. Their trenches, dug in chalk, were soundly built, clean and dry, unlike the sodden positions previously occupied by the battalion in the Ypres area.

The morning of 13 October found the battalion tense and waiting eagerly for the bombardment to start prior to the assault. When it did, at midday, it was far from the overwhelming cannonade prom-ised by the corps commander. After an hour came the release of gas and smoke clouds as a generous issue of rum was handed out to stiffen the resolve of the assaulting troops. When the gas ran out after less than an hour the Germans opened heavy fire on the British parapets; they were clearly ready to withstand the attack. Zero hour was at 2 p.m. As the barrage, such as it was, lifted onto the German reserve trenches, the Leicesters swarmed over the top, Colonel Martin at their head, together with the rest of 138 Brigade – the 5th Lincolns, followed by the second wave of the 4th Lincolns and 1st Monmouths, the divisional pioneer battalion. They were met at once by a tornado of machine gun fire and the German artillery's counter-barrage, and whole ranks of men were mown down even before reaching the

German wire, which was still largely uncut; but the attack was pressed home vigorously and the redoubt retaken. The advance continued despite appalling casualties and the next German strongpoint, Fosse 8, an elongated slag heap, was attacked. By now German resistance was furious and machine guns raked the advancing infantry from both flanks as they struggled on. The 4th Leicesters saw their CO fall seriously wounded. The Adjutant was dead and all the company commanders down. The second-in-command ran forward to assume command but he too fell, badly wounded, amidst the German wire. All order was now lost as innumerable hand-to-hand brawls broke out in the redoubt, where units rapidly became hopelessly inter-mingled. Ammunition and grenades soon ran out and there were no fatigue parties to bring up more supplies. The shattered remnants of the brigade began to fall back to their start line, and the redoubt was soon empty of all but dead and dying British infantry.

No Man's Land was a shambles; Colonel Martin, though severely wounded, lay in the front line trench to which he had been carried and from which the attack had been launched. He was still conscious and in command but unable to move. When not receiving reports and issuing new orders he read from his Bible to a young officer who lay dying beside him. Martin, though in great pain, stayed in the forward trench until ordered to the aid post by the brigade commander 24 hours after the start of the attack, of which the official history comments that: 'The fighting on the 13th and 14th of October had not improved the general situation in any way and had brought nothing but useless slaughter of the infantry'. The 46th Division had lost 180 officers and 3,583 men in the attack.

Every officer of the 4th Leicesters – 20 of them – who took part in that attack had become a casualty and only 188 NCOs and men answered the roll-call next day when the battalion mustered; 453 of all ranks had been killed or wounded. Among these would have been most of Kenneth's old platoon, the rough men for whom he had developed such affection. His friend Sergeant Major Bromley was among the wounded. The battalion history notes that '. . . the Quartermaster and the Transport Officer mess together alone, but they dare not look at each other'. They were the only unscathed officers surviving of the battalion that had embarked so cheerfully for France seven months earlier.

The increasingly cynical spirit of the time is reflected vividly in an anonymous poem quoted in the battalion's unofficial history *Footprints of the Fourth Leicestershire Regiment*, by one of its officers, Captain John Milne:

RIP (4th Leicesters)
From Kemmel Hill to Belleglise, from Lens to Dickebusche,
Through all the gory gamut, from 'Inspection' unto 'push'.
In perils oft, in weariness, in trenches and in rum,
They waged the war to end all war until Thy Kingdom Come.

From laughter loud to dark despair, from 'leave' to 'listening post',
From lusty life at Zero hour to puking up the ghost,
In agony and bloody sweat they paid the utmost sum,
To sleep the sleep that ends all sleep until Thy Kingdom Come.

Kenneth Dalgliesh, in later years, counted himself fortunate indeed to have escaped that slaughter, albeit with an empty sleeve as a reminder of his service. His emotions as he learnt of the loss of his comrades can scarcely be imagined.

The first intimations of this tragedy came to the city of Leicester as individual families received the dreaded telegram informing them that their husbands, brothers and sons were either wounded, missing or killed in action. The full measure of the disaster was apparent to all when the local newspaper, the *Leicester Daily Mercury*, carried a report that plunged the city into mourning:

It is with profound regret that we have to confirm the rumours that have been so persistently in circulation in the last few days, that the 1st/4th Leicesters have suffered severe losses. The battalion was in action on October 13, and how they suffered may be judged from the list of officers whose deaths have been officially notified to their relatives. The receipt of the news yesterday caused a painful sensation in the town, and the sympathy of all will go out to the relatives of those who have fallen. It is impossible at present to obtain anything like a complete list of the casualties among non-commissioned officers and men.

The battalion took many months to recover from this catastrophe. It took part in the Battle of the Somme when the 46th Division was given a subordinate and diversionary role on the fringe of the main attack on 1 July 1916, an event characterised by much confusion in which most of the troops involved were back in their own trenches within 30 minutes of the start of the attack. Due to inexperience and lack of rehearsal one brigade lost direction and blundered around in the dense smoke clouds discharged in an effort to shield the assaulting troops, and slowness off the start lines coupled by a leisurely pace of advance gave the German defenders plenty of time in which to leave their deep dugouts and man the parapet with machine guns. After this debacle the divisional commander, Major General Stuart-Wortley, was removed. Not until September 1918, as part of the overwhelming victory gained by a revived British Army did the now experienced 46th Division recover its form as it crossed the St Quentin Canal and broke into the formidable Hindenburg Line, when the 4th Leicesters were at last given the chance to show their mettle. By then, Kenneth Dalgliesh had found new avenues for his talents and the future that was to shape his life. But he never forgot his friends of the 4th Battalion.

The loss of his left arm he had accepted philosophically; after all, it would not be an insuperable disability to a right-handed architect, although there were times, particularly when he was stationed in Egypt later in the war, when he was given to pessimism that sometimes emerged in his letters home. He might have sought release from the Army on medical grounds but, like thousands of similarly war-damaged young men, was fully prepared to soldier on if suitable employment could be found for him. Many of those who had lost limbs or an eye were more than ready to accept posts in establishments training the New Armies or as staff officers in the United Kingdom and abroad. He was therefore pleased when a medical board pronounced him as 'fit for light duty' in January 1916.

By March he was back on duty, this time with a newly-raised reserve battalion of the Leicesters, the 3rd/4th, based at Nottingham where he was billeted at the George Hotel. To his great joy, he found himself serving once more with Sergeant Major Bromley, who had recovered from his wounds and was medically boarded as fit for home service only. In letters to his parents Kenneth described his new surroundings and the training of recruits. The men he was instructing were raw but keen; he described their reaction to vaccinations, a feature of military life to which few of them would have been accustomed. His talks on life at the Front, based on notes he had made while with the 1st/4th Battalion, were listened to attentively by the recruits.

Aerial attacks were now being made on the United Kingdom by German airships or Zeppelins. Although the physical effects of the bombing were negligible compared to those of the Second World War, Kenneth mentions the alarm of the citizens of Nottingham to one such scare while he was out of town at Beeston. The bus on which he attempted to return to Nottingham was stopped by police so he commandeered a four-seater car and was driven back to camp.

In April he was still at the George Hotel training the new battalion. He noted with distaste disciplinary methods, routine in the old Regular Army, still being unimaginatively applied to recruits by the older officers and NCOs, often with negative effect. Kenneth reported a 'minor mutiny' in his company, triggered by the award of extra pack drill by the Quartermaster when some of the recruits failed to respond to reveille; after seven hours of this punishment it is hardly surprising that there was resentment. Unperceived by many of the older regulars the British Army was now a citizen force whose members would not respond to time-honoured methods of enforcing discipline. Kenneth was quick to see that these were inappropriate for citizen soldiers:

The recruits were posted to my company and I found it of absorbing interest to build up from the raw material, not only from the drill point of view but from the psychological aspect. The men were all of such different characters; some could be moulded, some led, others guided, and a very few with whom one could do nothing at all, but it was very rare to find one completely unresponsive – I think I can only remember one – and I just had to keep him constantly in the guard room. In fact, he was sent out to France in handcuffs. We shook hands before the train went out and he asked me if he could have the bracelets off, but I knew perfectly well that he would bolt at the first opportunity. It was hard to refuse.

The thing that always distressed me was having to put men in the guardroom for overstaying their draft leave. Such decent fellows and one knew they would come back to duty and would as gladly have forgiven them – but there it is, war is war and discipline cannot be relaxed. I always put a few packets of cigarettes in my pocket when I was Duty Officer, but I hated visiting them in the cells.

The Nottingham letters cease with one dated 21 April 1916 and the correspondence reopens in September, from Egypt. During the intervening months Kenneth, finding the routine at Nottingham boring, was delighted when the unit was transferred to Catterick in Yorkshire, where he and Sergeant Major Bromley were able to go for long walks on the moors when off duty. By the time he embarked on the troopship bound for the eastern Mediterranean he was fit and increasingly untroubled by the loss of his left arm.

7

THE CENSOR OF PORT SAID

Britain had deployed an army in Egypt since 1882 when it appeared essential to secure the Suez Canal as the arterial route linking Britain with the Indian Empire and its other possessions and dominions further east. In 1914 it was Britain's most important single strategic asset, particularly in the light of Germany's evident aim of establishing a sphere of interest across the Arab world and ultimately, it was felt, of displacing British influence in the Middle and Far East. For some time therefore, Germany had been wooing the Ottoman Empire, now in terminal decline. The grandiose Berlin-to-Baghdad railway scheme was underway and enormous amounts of German aid had been poured into the Turkish economy. A formidable German training team had been sent to Constantinople in 1913 with the mission of reforming the Ottoman Army following its failure in a succession of Balkan wars and in the former Ottoman province of Libya where the Italians had defeated it in 1912. Political power in Turkey was slipping from the hands of the Sultan and his advisers with the emergence of a new political movement under the leadership of what were known as the Young Turks and it was they, under the charismatic Enver Pasha, who steadily undermined the old regime and ensured continuing German support. The Germans, however, had a different agenda, which they considered could best be achieved by enlisting Turkish support as they fulfilled their plan to cut Britain's access to the Indian Empire and to Australia and New Zealand by seizing the Suez Canal and encouraging the Muslim world to rise against British influence throughout the Middle East. This aim would be attained by getting the Ottoman Sultan – who was also the Caliph of all Islam and nominal spiritual and temporal leader of all citizens of his empire – to proclaim a *jihad* against the infidel. (One subsidiary aim of this was that there would be widespread mutinies in the predominantly Muslim regiments of the Indian Army such as the Punjabi and Frontier Force units; in the event they were to fight valiantly for the Raj on many fronts.)

As the bounds of the Ottoman Empire extended to Palestine and the Sinai, right down the Arabian peninsula almost to Aden, and in Mesopotamia to the mouths of the Tigris and Euphrates, where the strategically vulnerable oil terminals of the Anglo-Persian Petroleum Company were sited, the security of Egypt, the Canal Zone and the vital coaling station of Aden demanded maximum security. An expeditionary force was despatched from India to secure the oil terminals, pipelines and up-country oil wells and slowly advanced up the two great rivers towards Baghdad, initiating the Mesopotamian Campaign.

The general officer commanding in Egypt on the outbreak of war in 1914 was General Sir John Maxwell. Almost at once the regular army garrisons were withdrawn and replaced by Territorials from England. As a further precaution, the Australian and New Zealand Army Corps, intended for the Western Front, was disembarked in Egypt, ostensibly to complete its collective training but in fact to stiffen the garrison against the perceived threat to the canal from Sinai where a considerable Turkish build-up had been detected following Turkey's entry into the war on the side of Germany in November 1914. This threat soon materialised. In January 1915, following an arduous march across the wastes of the Sinai desert, a Turkish force some 20,000 strong attempted to cross the canal using prefabricated pontoons. The attack was repelled with the aid of British and French warships and the Turks retired in commendably good order back into Palestine. Maxwell reacted by moving his forward defences across the canal and into the Sinai to forestall any subsequent Turkish attempts and his prudence was justified when the next effort was made in August 1916. By now the Egyptian garrison had been strengthened; lines of outposts extended some way into the desert and construction of pipelines for water and fuel, together with light railways, had begun to edge up the Mediterranenean coast towards Palestine.

By mid-September 1916 Kenneth was in Egypt, writing about the squalor of the villages and the gangs of labourers under supervisors who freely used the lash to increase the work rate. This, and other scenes, he illustrated graphically in sketches – the first of many in the following months. He had an enquiring mind and great curiosity, sketching anything that interested him, such as Arab dhows, or '. . . a most peculiar tree'. Later that month, while awaiting a suitable staff post, he appears to have spent some time on a passenger ship, the SS *Transylvania,* in the Mediterranean during which he visited Malta before disembarking at Salonika, where an Allied force had been based since the late summer of 1915 in a belated effort to relieve pressure on Serbia, resulting in what soon became an embarrassing, costly and generally ineffective Anglo-French enclave which not only failed to save the Serbs from defeat and occupation by the Austro-German and Bulgarian Armies but tied up considerable Allied resources. Although the censorship forbade mention of actual places, Kenneth's vivid descriptions of both Malta and Salonika indicate that he spent a short time in both.

At Salonika he was impressed by the architecture of the Byzantine churches and Ottoman mosques:

You would like the churches and mosques – one church, St Demetrius, has most wonderful old second- and third-century mosaics; they are mostly circular churches with sort of misericord seats round the walls, and are mostly spoilt by glass chandeliers. St Demetrius has the reputed tomb of that saint, in a dark evil smelling chapel with no windows, lit by offertory candles and a Greek priest in attendance . . . There is an old wall round most of the town that is supposed to have been built by Constantine and an old triumphal arch with Roman bas-relief carving all over the base . . . any amount of Turks and Moslems, they wear very baggy breeches with a huge seat hanging down to the knees. It is a religious belief that to a Cretan man a messiah will be born some day, so they wear the enormous seat to the breeches in case of accident!

By the middle of October he was back in Egypt, having sailed from Salonika on the *Transylvania*; his letters are now headed 'GHQ Egyptian Expeditionary Force', full of well-observed comment on the unfamiliar scenes around him. German submarines were active in the Mediterranean and in a letter home of 13 October Kenneth reported the loss of the Cunarder *Franconia*, torpedoed between Alexandria and Malta: '. . . they only lost seven. The *Dover Castle* picked them up, and brought them here, all in the clothes they stood up in – cooks, stewards, officers, and a puppy . . .'

After landing at Alexandria Kenneth went by train to GHQ at Ismailia on the Suez Canal, keeping his parents up to date in thinly veiled words:

> Of course I must be very strict, being a Censor, and must not do what I can't allow others to do (the news I have given you up to the present is all past and doesn't matter). Do you remember where George Anderson was? Well. I'm not there, but quite close. There is very little to see here – sand and water and palms – and absolutely nothing to do. I am at present in the Chief Censor's Office for instruction and shall then be sent away on my own – Alex, Port Said, Cairo. He asked me where I would like to go and I told him somewhere with a certain degree of comfort as my days of roughing it are over.

Huge military bases existed around Alexandria and Cairo and along the banks of the canal. The end of the Gallipoli Campaign early in January 1916 had resulted in the transfer of thousands of troops from there to the Canal Zone and Salonika, the arrival of great numbers of headquarters and administrative personnel and the setting-up of the necessary medical and hospital services. Port Said, at the Mediterranean entrance to the Suez Canal, was a major logistic

John F. Kerr
Pt Said
Nov 1916

Portrait by KD of Lt John Kerr, one of his fellow censors at Port Said, who had lost
a leg on the Western Front earlier in the war but had also opted to continue in service.

base and Kenneth found that he would be posted there on completion of his Censor's training. Meanwhile he continued to explore around GHQ. With a keen interest in calligraphy of all sorts he was fascinated by the Arabs' skill in this and by the intricacy and beauty of the inscriptions to be seen in and around mosques, some of which he copied meticulously. Specimens of his efforts decorate some of his letters home (with the added remark 'I haven't got hold of it properly yet . . .'). He was joined at the Censor's Office in Port Said by kindred spirits who, like him, had received wounds barring them from further combat but still capable of light duties. One, whom he had met some months earlier in hospital at Brighton, is initially referred to as 'Kerr' (the undue use of Christian names being thought over-familiar by these Edwardians). Kerr, an officer in one of the Lowland Scottish regiments, had lost a leg in France

'Three legs, three arms' – KD's own caption for this photograph taken when he and Lt John ('Silas') Kerr were on leave in Cairo following the completion of their Censors' training at GHQ.

but, like Kenneth, was determined not to let this impair his enjoyment of life. The two of them, before leaving Cairo for Port Said on completion of their training as Censors, went off in a hired car to see the pyramids and the sphinx, where they were photographed mounted on camels. Kenneth's interest was stimulated by the sight of Arab stonecutters at work near the great monuments and he sketched them.

Like millions of tourists in Egypt he succumbed to the lure of the bazaar, buying presents for the family at home. Unlike the majority he had an architect's insight, marvelling at the splendour of Islamic buildings in Cairo and the ingenuity of their structures, noting that the Mosque of Mehmet Ali ('tawdry apart from its alabaster') bore a striking resemblance to the Agia Sofia in Constantinople, that great mosque, formerly Christian cathedral, on whose tremendous dome the Muslim builders had based their design. At the end of October he was sending photographs home with his letters and complaining that he had received no mail from home since leaving England in mid-September. In their last few days of leisure before leaving Cairo for Port Said he and Kerr amused themselves by haggling with traders at their hotel, or watching the 'gulli-gulli' man or street conjurer. At the Cairo Zoo he noted approvingly that the animals were in good condition, admired some beautiful gardens, and watched the Nile flooding to 22 feet above its normal level.

On 5 November Kenneth and Kerr paid a last visit to the bazaar. Watching the religious procession of the Holy Carpet associated with the Muslim *Hajj* season, Kenneth comments on the bearing of the Egyptian Guard of Honour in words of almost comical political incorrectness (that is, by the standards of the early twenty-first century): 'I expect they were Sudanese as they are finer men than Gippies . . . I hate the Egyptians, they are damned low dirty thieving lot of swines.' Next day the two Censors were off to Port Said by train, departing at 11 a.m., via Zagazig and Ismailia. Arriving at their destination they were accommodated at a hotel on the waterfront close to the De Lesseps statue, erected shortly after the opening of the canal near the harbour entrance, pointing dramatically towards the east in the direction of Port Suez. (After the Allied landings at Port Said in November 1956 an unknown Royal Marine climbed the statue and placed a green Commando beret on its head. Following the ignominious Anglo-French withdrawal the Egyptians, having failed to remove the beret – which had apparently been cemented in position – decided to blow De Lesseps up and the canal lost a world-famous landmark as a result.)

The two officers quickly found their hotel '. . . abominable, food none too good, service damnable, 10 shillings a day – so we'll look for a flat'. Their workplace was already established at the General Post Office, with a postal address of 'Base Censor, Port Said, Egypt'. On 9 November Kenneth was describing their daily routine as they ploughed through the outgoing mail, of which there was vast heaps: '. . . great black buck niggers in uniform . . . bring us bundles of

'The Censors of Port Said'. Although KD depicts himself here equipped with a standard issue hook, he seems to have soon abandoned it. These three officers, all rendered unfit for further combat duties by reason of their wounds, lived together amicably in a flat in Port Said. Curiously, Kenneth has portrayed them all wearing their Sam Browne cross strap on the left and not the right (correct) shoulder.

letters . . .'. He also mentions that the hotel was filling up with survivors from the liner *Arabia*, recently torpedoed by one of the increasing number of U-boats operating in the Mediterranean from bases on the Austrian Adriatic coast.

The day's routine appears none too strenuous:

> . . . get to the office at 9 a.m. and work solidly till nearly 1 o'clock . . . we lunch at 1 and return to the office and work till between 4 & 5 when we usually go along to a neighbouring hotel and have tea (on the pavement). Little boys come and badger us to have our boots cleaned and we say '*Imshi Allah*'. After tea we often go for a sail in the harbour – they are of course native Arab boats with one big sail and are topping little things to handle. It is usually moonlight when we return as it is practically dark here at 5.30 p.m. After our sail we stroll back to the hotel and sit in the street and eat baked peanuts and watch the people go by, until 7 o'clock when we toddle back to our own hotel. The peanuts are awfully good, just ordinary monkey nuts baked and salted. After dinner we light our pipes and sit out on the breakwater by De Lesseps statue and talk, and finally turn in around 9.30 or 10 o'clock. Don't think we are getting too frequent in our visits to the hotels, dear old people, for I don't think I have drunk more than a dozen or so whisky & sodas since I have been in Egypt – it doesn't suit me a bit. Here, I hardly ever have anything but quinine tonic water, either for dinner or luncheon. I am practically a teetotaller here.

Kenneth had been determined from the start to ignore the loss of his left arm and wasted no time on self-sympathy. Very few day-to-day tasks, such as lighting his pipe, caused problems as he quickly acquired the dexterity to do them single-handed. He had always enjoyed riding and was delighted to be able to pursue this at Port Said:

There is a man here who has a very fine three-year-old pony stallion which he lends me. I take him down to the sea shore and we have some topping canters on the sands. He is the most beautiful little horse I have ever ridden, he prances along on his toes and is just like being on a spring mattress.

It was time to move from the hotel into a flat and Kenneth and his friend Captain Kerr had to choose their domestic staff, starting with a Sudanese cook. Having selected the most likely candidate they embarked on the chores of housekeeping. Kenneth sent a sketch of the floor plan of the flat to his parents; it shows it to have had a balcony overlooking a busy street, four bedrooms, a dining room, kitchen and small bathroom. News had evidently arrived at Port Said of the torpedoing of the ship carrying home-bound mails, for Kenneth added a postscript to his letter: 'I will now endeavour to rewrite the letter that is lying at the bottom of the sea!! Damn the Hun!! All my love, dear old people, God Bless you all, Ken.'

Following the Turkish attempt to cross the canal early in 1915 and its repulse, the campaign for the defence of Egypt was conducted at a low pitch for the rest of the year and into 1916. The Turks retired back into Palestine across the Sinai Desert and the British High Command was content to make a cautious advance along the Mediterranean coast across the canal in order to forestall any further Turkish offensive operations. Operations flared up briefly in April and again, this time rather more dangerously, in August, when a two-day engagement was fought near the coast at Romani, east of the canal and north of Ismailia, no more than 35 miles from Port Said. In this fighting the Australian Light Horse Brigade, which had spent the previous year as infantry at Gallipoli, performed with outstanding dash under its commander General Chauvel. By the time Kenneth arrived in Egypt the fighting had died down but it was clear that the front needed to be shifted forward, up to a hundred miles along the coastal strip to the area of Gaza, to safeguard the Egyptian base and the canal. A deliberate forward move was therefore undertaken, with roads, pipelines

The view from the balcony of the flat shared by Kenneth Dalgliesh, John Kerr and John Wayet.

101

and a railway following in the wake of the advance up the coastal strip.

While these operations were in train, a further threat to Egypt had arisen on its western frontier with what is now Libya where dissident tribes backed by German and Turkish agents had rallied under the Grand Senussi of Sollum. A running guerrilla campaign was fought in the western deserts – to be the scene of major battles in the Second World War – as a scratch force assembled by GOC (General Officer Commanding) Egypt chased an elusive and skilful enemy for almost two more years.

Although the garrison of Egypt had been swollen considerably early in 1916 by the evacuation of Gallipoli, these assets were steadily eroded by the need to send as many reinforcements as possible to Salonika and to the Western Front, where matters had remained critical through 1915, and there were times when the British GHQ staff would have been distinctly worried that a stronger Turkish offensive, if delivered towards the end of 1916, might indeed succeed in cutting the canal and overrunning the defence. None of these worries appears to have troubled Kenneth; or at least there is no sign of this in his letters home, which continue in an optimistic vein.

The two Censors had been joined in their flat by a third member of the team, Captain Wayet of the Lincolnshire Regiment, who is first mentioned as being hospitalised with malaria:

. . . a very nice fellow. He and his brother were farmers in Lincolnshire before the war – had three farms and did very well. His brother, poor chap, has been killed. I am seriously thinking of joining him after the war as he wants someone to take his brother's place . . . he is going to join us in the flat when he comes out of hospital . . . we are living in fine style on about 10/- per day for the three of us. We draw our Army rations (meat, veg, tea, sugar, salt, pepper, jam, cheese, mustard and baccy) instead of drawing 1/7d a day and then our servant the black boy buys fish and a few extras. The cook is quite

Fellow Censor John Wayet.

good and he fries soles to perfection . . . we have a very fine old Sudanese watchman who also works the lift. His name is Osman and he bosses all the blacks in this block of flats – they absolutely daren't do wrong as he would kill them if they did. Osman is a very fine old man, very faithful and trustworthy, whenever he sees us he rises *slowly* to his feet, salutes, and a large smile *slowly* appears over his face and then *slowly* fades away. He is like a big black idol – on weekdays he wears a white gown and turban, on Sundays a large black gown . . .

Kenneth's admiration for Osman and other Sudanese did not extend to the general Egyptian population, described in terms that would make any liberal soul quail – but his views were certainly shared at the time by virtually every member of the armed forces stationed in Egypt:

You must not get too good an idea of the natives out here. The average Sudanese like Osman is very faithful and a decent chap but the Egyptians are a rotten low crowd. I don't wonder Pharo [*sic*] oppressed them. They pray hard & that's about all they do. They steal and lie and are not to be trusted at all . . .

His parents kept Kenneth informed about various mutual acquaintances at home, and asked for his views from time to time on aspects of military discipline, particularly when some radical Member of Parliament had raised this issue in the House:

Yes, I know that man (Mrs Aslett's brother) had been cashiered, and the other one will be as well if he is not careful, they both drink like fishes. Blatchfield is a damned fool and doesn't know what he is talking about, most of these armchair critics are. To start with, 'crucifixion' means nailing or roping a man to a cross or tree with his feet clean off the ground so that his own weight tells. 'Tommy' is the average British soldier whom

'The Lighthouse, Port Said'. An example of KD's skill
as an architectural draughtsman.

we and all nations respect. What Blatchford speaks about is
what is known in the Army as Field Punishment No. 1. No
one has the power to impose this punishment in England, only
overseas in the field on active service (active service by the
way is when one is fighting for one's country, a somewhat
serious business). Field P No. 1 is given as a punishment for
very serious offences, to absolutely incorrigible men – men to
whom reason does not appeal – and though the case B. quotes
seems very sad I don't suppose he has for one moment got
at the really true facts of the case. He doesn't for one moment
realise what it is to command an army, or even a battalion, and
the absolute need for discipline. As I used to tell my men,
'Discipline is essential to success'. All men are not alike – B.
seems to think so and that they are all jolly fine fellows. Yes
I have seen FP No. 1 in France. I saw the men tied up one
day – in fact several times. I have seen it – the battalion is
paraded and it is not by any means a pleasant sight, nor are
decayed corpses or men with their brains in their hats, but it's
all part of war and all its terribleness. Don't think I am callous,
I'm not in the least, but it does make me wild when some
damned fools (meaning Blatchford of course) talk about things
they know nothing about. I ought to explain that when men
are tied up, they are tied up to a gun wheel (legs and arms) or
a tree, and their feet are not off the ground. If that question
is ever asked in the House, let us hope there will be someone
to tell them the true facts of FP No. 1 . . . Now I must stop,
we have just finished dinner (soup, fish, meat, cheese savoury,
and a bottle of Graves – NB no tonic water available!) and
are going to a concert at the local cinema. These concerts are
given by Tommies and sailors and are usually very good.

Good night dearest people, God bless you all, Ken.

8

NEW HORIZONS

The mails were continually affected by frequent torpedoing of Allied shipping in the Mediterranean and early in December 1916 Kenneth reported that he believed several of his letters home had been lost when the *Arabia* was sunk. Although not mentioned in his letters at this stage he was clearly aware of the nursing Sisters who were working either ashore in base hospitals in Port Said or on the hospital ships, several of which seem to have been torpedoed indiscriminately, 'quite regardless as to whether they are hospital ships or not, damn their souls, to think of risking all those dear nurses' lives'. Despite these losses the mails were remarkably speedy – letters posted in England as late as 25 November arrived in Port Said by 9 December.

One of Kenneth's colleagues in the Censor's Office, Captain Wayet, had fallen sick again with malaria early in December and as the hospital was on the other side of the harbour it was necessary to visit him by boat:

Latterly I have taken to sailing across – the night before last the harbour was like a mill pond – I had to go down to the Sherif Basin to collect a parcel. There was very little wind and I glided along in the moonlight by the coal barges where the Arabs were crooning a little song to themselves . . . it is topping in the harbour on a moonlit night – practically no traffic. I am getting quite a good hand at sailing these native boats – I tear along at full speed up to the landing stage – then turn her suddenly into the wind and the sails go jibber jab – slapper slop – and we glide slowly in . . .

Writing on 9 December, Kenneth was able to report, in none too favourable terms, on his encounter with one of the most celebrated figures of naval aviation when he attended a tea party held by Mrs Cave, the wife of the Assistant Provost Marshal. The officer in question had distinguished himself in the Dardanelles when commanding the Royal Naval Air Service (RNAS) detachments there but was already noted for his ferocious temper, bristling ginger beard and shortness of stature:

It was rather a disappointing afternoon as Commander Samson came in, and he is such an utter pig. John and I just sat still and prayed for him to go and when he did he just walked out. One would have thought he would have had the decency to say 'well, goodbye you fellows', even if only out of courtesy to Mrs Cave's guests. He is a swine . . .

Samson was to earn further laurels later in the war when commanding a RNAS armoured car unit sent to Russia, and is regarded as a founding father of what eventually became the Fleet Air Arm.

A bound handwritten copy of the Koran that Kenneth had bought in the Cairo market turned out to be something of a find; he had it valued in Port Said by an Egyptian expert:

. . . who knows all about them and he says if it was bought for £5 it was a bargain, I was told it is worth between £15 and £20 – I paid 11/-!! It is 62 years old. The finis note says 'We thank God for the finishing of His Holy Book and we pray Him to be merciful to our Prophet Mohamad and all his relations & friends. It was written by the poor servant who is weaker than the ant, Sayedd Mohamad El Hikmany, one of the pupils of Ahmad El Nazifi, El Haggi who has learnt the Koran. God forgive their sins and cover their mistakes. Written in 1275 Hag.' There – isn't that nice? When I get back I am going to have it repaired by a good man.

The threat posed by U-boats in the Mediterranean had now assumed major proportions. In addition to large boats entering the Mediterranean via the Straits of Gibraltar, smaller ones were being assembled in the Austro-Hungarian Navy's Adriatic bases from parts prefabricated in Germany, and the failure of a string of nets across the narrows at the foot of the Adriatic (the Otranto Barrage), to prevent their entry into the eastern Mediterranean and Aegean Sea, led to very serious shipping losses by mid-1916. Kenneth was well aware of the effect of this on the mail and informed his parents that henceforth he would not be sending anything other than letters: 'it is dangerous to send *things* home, there is no reason why one shouldn't send a cheque, for if the Huns torpedo it I can easily write another . . .'. He was also prone to philosophising on the strange circumstances forced upon him by the war:

> . . . I often think of the days and years spent in that Fenchurch Street office and there's old Meaden mugging away day after day, year after year and seeing nothing and here am I, I've been in the trenches, I've fired a rifle with intent to kill, and been plugged for my trouble and now I've been all along the Mediterranean from one end to the other and up and down the Greek archipelago . . . and now I am in Egypt.

Throughout the previous year the Turkish government had carried out an appalling persecution of its Armenian population, using the pretext that they had taken part in attacks on Ottoman troops engaged in the abortive campaign in the Caucasus in the late autumn of 1914, when supply columns of the Turkish Army had been ambushed by Armenian guerrillas. The exact figures will never be known but it is possible that almost a million Armenians, men, women and children alike, were slaughtered or left to die in the open. Refugees were brought to Egypt and other centres and a huge camp established for them outside Port Said. Kenneth visited it just before Christmas 1916; his opinions would be unpalatable and downright heartless now to many but he was a man of his time, instinctively repelled by certain types of foreigner. He clearly bracketed the hapless Armenians with the Egyptians:

> I went up to the Armenian refugee camp the other afternoon. There are about 5,000 of them here and they make mats and lace and any amount of confectionery – it is very interesting to see them at work but they are a lazy and ungrateful lot, and I don't blame the Turks for massacring them, it's a pity they didn't complete the job.

Christmas of 1916 came and went uneventfully in Port Said. Kenneth had continued to enjoy his sailing, and had taken some of the nursing Sisters from the Stationary Hospital out in a motor launch; the first of many such excursions.

Following a steady build-up of forces in Egypt the Expeditionary Force was poised to advance into Palestine. There had to be a major logistic prelude; huge dumps were established in the Canal Zone. Roads and a railway were now extended up the Mediterranean coast towards the Egyptian border with Palestine, together with fuel and water pipelines. By April 1917 these were nearing the Palestine border despite stiffening opposition as preparations were completed for the land offensive to expel the Ottomans from the Holy Land. General Sir Archibald Murray, Maxwell's successor as Commander in Chief, delegated the conduct of the advance to Major General Sir Charles Dobell whose start-line was at El Arish, 30 miles from the frontier where the Turks were firmly dug in. Dobell knew that his main problem was water; he had a large mounted force under his command and it was essential to seize the wells at Gaza if the 10,000 horses of General Chetwode's 'Desert Column' of Yeomanry and Australian Light Horse were to be watered and sustained in the field. Gaza was therefore the objective for the advance. The First Battle of Gaza began on 26 March 1917 with an infantry advance. Initially things went according to plan but the cavalry, whose role was to turn the Turkish inland flank, soon ran out of water and had to be recalled. The frontal infantry assault was thrown back with heavy casualties. Dobell called off the attack and had to rethink his tactics.

A sudden and unexpected workload was imposed on the medical services at the Egyptian base as a result of this battle and, in anticipation of similar losses when the attack was resumed, large numbers of doctors and nursing staff were sent out from the United Kingdom to reinforce the medical services. While these events were taking place, the Censor's Office at Port Said continued its steady if unexciting work. Kenneth's letters reflect the mood in the base as well as casting an interesting light on its lively social life.

The intensification of the campaign in Palestine had greatly increased the size of the medical services, bringing many more nurses of the Queen Alexandra's Imperial Military Nursing Service (QAIMNS) to Egypt to reinforce those who had been in the operational theatre since early in the war. Among these was Sister Ellen Constance Franklin. Aged 32 in 1916, she had trained and qualified as a State Registered Nurse (SRN) at Southampton General Hospital. This enabled her to volunteer in 1914 for war service as a nursing Sister in the reserve of the QAIMNS, into which she was commissioned shortly after the outbreak of war. By the time of the Armistice in 1918 she would have served in Egypt, at Salonika, aboard hospital ships in the Aegean and off the Dardanelles, and on board a ship bound for Bombay carrying wounded and sick sepoys of the Indian Army back home. Her war service would be recognised by the award of the Royal Red Cross 2nd Class in 1917 and – unusually – a mention in despatches 'in recognition of valuable services with the Armies in the Field' as notified in General Murray's official despatch of 1 December 1916. By the end of the war she had earned the right to wear the 1915 Star, British War and Victory medals (known by all veterans of the war as 'Pip, Squeak and Wilfred' after a trio of well known cartoon characters of the day). She was destined to change the life of Kenneth Dalgliesh of the Leicestershire Regiment.

The steady stream of letters home continued. Kenneth saluted his parents on New Year's Day 1917:

Dear old people,

Here's wishing you all a very Happy New Year. Many thanks for the letter from old home of the 10th December, I haven't had any others from you since then . . . I am enclosing a couple of photos of Ken sailing. The man with me is my angular Arab boatman, known universally as 'John Sullivan'. He is a very good sailor and doesn't lose an ounce of wind if he can help it, moreover his boat is almost the fastest in the harbour. I have got my leg over the tiller to rest my arm a bit as she was pulling somewhat – I didn't know I was being taken at that moment. I had a topping sail this morning, the sea is very rough and we got soused but it was fine in the sun and wind, when I came back my face was coated with salt . . . I was afraid John Sullivan didn't love me very much as he had no overcoat and got drenched to the skin. His little brother (who is chiefly employed in climbing up the sail) thought it an over-rated pastime and crept into a small locker in the bows, I really felt a bit sorry for them, we were getting such a pitching and rolling and a big rattle of sea every few minutes . . . I expect you think I'm doing a lot of sailing and not much work. Well you see we are quite slack at present and we take it in turns to have mornings and afternoons off . . . There is a little show over at the hospital tonight, given by the nurses. I think I shall look in . . .

Best love dear old people, God Bless you all, Ken.

Determined not to waste his time off duty, Kenneth embarked on the study of ancient history, particularly that of the Bible and of the country in which he was serving. He was also taking French lessons:

My French mistress is a very charming girl (she *would* be, eh!). She is a Montenegrin and lives with her mother. Her father was the Montenegrin attaché in England. The name, by the way, is

'There is a little show over at the hospital tonight, given by the nurses – I think I shall look in . . .' This appears to be the entertainment to which Kenneth refers; a grand patriotic display. The figure disguised as a pack of cards (top right) has been identified as Sister Franklin.

Ilinka Gosdenovich. When the war broke out they were in Montenegro and had to leave their home at an hour's notice and fly for their lives . . . One has to speak French a great deal here, if one's going to be at all social. On Saturday evenings most of the little girls that one dances with are French and I go and talk to their Mammas and they say 'Monsieur Dalgliesh is a very nice man' and then I dance with their sweet daughters (and sit out with them!), *c'est tres drolles*. Kerr and Wayet are too nervous to tackle French so I steal a march on them. On Sunday mornings they say 'Kenneth, you seemed to be having rather a good time last night – what was she like?' and I say 'Oh – she's a sweet thing but she can't speak a word of English!'

The three officers enjoyed life despite the shortcomings of their locally-recruited servants, who had to be replaced frequently, either for uncleanliness, absence, dishonesty or sheer incompetence. Kenneth's opinion of the Egyptians continued to be low; he reported in one letter of the way in which the gang leader of a party of street cleaners belaboured his men with an umbrella until the arrival of a policeman who chastised him in turn:

> The Gyppies are a rum lot. Last Saturday we were going to the casino Palace for dinner and the Gharry was rather crowded with Ken and his wooden leg, so I got on the box and drove the horses. The driver protested but I told him I would 'beat his brains out' so he sat quietly and I drove along and I said '*menak*' and '*shemallak*' to the pedestrians – 'Keep to the right' and 'Keep to the left'.

In his letters at Christmastide 1916 Kenneth failed to mention that he had been admitted to hospital earlier in December suffering from what he described as 'a boil on my BTM'. He was furious to discover that the military authorities had communicated this news to his parents and assured them at the end of January that he was fully recovered, having spent a week in hospital: '. . . well – we weren't busy and the nurses and everyone were so kind . . .'.

Back at home, Kenneth's parents were worried by his apparently negative attitude towards the local population and he reassured them by return of post:

> No, you dear old mother, of course I don't show my dislike to the natives, we just treat them like children. Talking about natives, Wayet and I declared war against the Postmaster's secretary the other afternoon. He is a very jolly chap, quite one of the best Gyppies I have met, and he thoroughly enjoys a joke. We stole his electric light and waste paper basket and when he came to claim them we bombed him with empty tobacco tins and his own waste paper basket which by the way was full to the brim . . .

Throughout 1916 a sporadic but frequently hard-fought campaign had continued in the deserts on the western Egyptian frontier where the Senussi continued to harass the Anglo-Egyptian forces, aided by German and Turkish military advisers. Elsewhere in the theatre of war the Turks had inflicted a humiliating defeat on General Townshend at Kut-al-Amara in Mesopotamia, which would not be avenged until the arrival of substantial reinforcements and a new and energetic British commander, General Maude, which ensured the recapture of Kut in February 1917 and of Baghdad in the following month. Port Said teemed with military activity as reinforcements swelled the garrison of Egypt. Kenneth still kept in touch with his few surviving friends in the 1st/4th Leicesters in France and was intrigued to find that the sniper who had put him out of action was dealt with shortly thereafter:

> ... he wasn't a bad sort of Boche for he helped me to a hundred a year [a reference to the £100 a year pension initially granted for the loss of his left arm] and many new and nice friends. He's dead now, poor old hoss, did I tell you he couldn't leave his sniping alone and our men got rather sick of it, so when the grass grew long a Sergeant crept out and killed him one day. I always think that was my particular Boche ...

Early in February 1917 Kenneth was given a chance to visit the Front; the railway, together with sealed roads and pipelines for fuel and water had been extended to El Arish, some 25 miles from the Palestinian border. Writing on 12 February he described his visit:

> I had a great time last week, I went to El Arish, the place where we had a big fight at Christmas. Some weeks ago I met a man in the Royal Engineers who was out in France with my division, the 46th, and who knew a lot of men that I know. He is at present stationed at Kantara and with his Major's permission we ran up to El Arish in the Major's private coach. I left here at 8.15 a.m. on Tuesday morning, 9.2.17., Dickson met me at Kantara. We crossed the canal to his lines and left there again by rail at 12.50 p.m. The coach is a large third-class

compartment fitted with two bunks, table, chairs, bathroom and kitchen so we travelled in comparative comfort. We passed thro' Romani, the place where we fought and turned the Turks in August 1916. After Romani, the wire marching road that the Turks laid started [he is referring to a mesh, a primitive form of the Somerfeld tracking widely used in the Second World War for aircraft runways]. It is a most wonderful invention for marching over the desert. A number of men walked along laying brushwood, then others came and laid down the wire (just ordinary rabbit wire) and then came their big guns – that is how it was laid, and now we march along it and fight them! I saw the desert really properly for the first time, sand, sand, sand, as far as the eye could reach. Sand hills in places, and great sand drifts. The old caravan route, hundreds and thousands of years old, runs along almost the whole way and must have been used by the Turks, for we passed several dead camels. It was quite easy to know when one was approaching a dead camel because of the smell. The further we went, the more fertile the desert became, if one could call it fertile at all. We reached El Arish about 8.45 p.m., 110 miles. After dinner in the coach Dickson and I went for a stroll up to the Sheikh's Tomb that stands on a small hill by the sea but it was so bitterly cold that we soon came back and turned in. I had my pyjamas and flea bag [a woollen sleeping bag, popular with officers on the Western Front; the best ones were made by the firm of Jaeger; I inherited my father's, used by him on the Somme in 1916 – it lasted me through my schooldays and saw service in Korea, 1950–1952 before the moths destroyed it in the late 1950s Ed] – but it was so cold I wished I had some blankets . . . I mustn't talk too much to you about El Arish or I shall have to censor my own letter. I'll tell you all about it after the war. Well, we left again at 10.20 a.m. and reached Kantara at 6.15 p.m. I had dinner in the RE Mess and caught the 10.10 p.m. down here arriving at 11.15 p.m., nearly 300 miles in all.

In March 1917 Kenneth was granted some leave, spending it on an expedition up the Nile to Luxor in the company of three nursing Sisters. In a letter dated 17 March he begins to describe the trip without revealing that one of them was Sister Franklin:

> Well you dear old people, since I wrote you last I have travelled nearly 1,600 miles, I have been up to Luxor and Assouan on a seven days' leave with three nurses, and oh, what a trip. I cannot attempt to describe it in this letter – I am still thinking about all the wonderful things I have seen – the Colossi at Thebes, the wonderful paintings on the tombs, the moonlight on the hills and mountains . . . Philae, the Assouan Dam *et al.* It cost me nearly a month's pay and I don't regret a farthing.

A fuller description of the holiday is given in a letter home dated 23 March:

> Well, I arrived at Luxor at 11.30 p.m. after fifteen hours in the train. I was met at the station by a sweet little nurse and drove to the Savoy Hotel where two more dear nurses awaited me!! We sat for an hour on the river terrace under a pergola covered with bougainvillaea, the hills curving away in the distance and the Nile at our feet, all in a lovely full moon. The Sisters had got hold of a very good guide and the next morning at 9.30 we crossed the river in a shaky old felucca and mounted our donkeys for a ride to Thebes . . .

With a trained eye for the wonders of the ancient buildings around him, Kenneth was able to describe what he saw with such accuracy that he could be writing in a tour guide book of the twenty-first century:

> We next visited the Ramasseum, a temple built by Rameses II and dedicated to Amen-Ra. It is impossible to describe all these temples, it would take too long – there is the Pylon, the

Second Court, the Hypostyle Hall . . . all the walls and pillars are covered with beautiful hieroglyphs. Here also is a colossal statue of Rameses, fallen and broken, all in polished black granite. It stood nearly 60 feet high, and all in one block of stone – the ear alone measures 3 feet 6 inches . . .

Elsewhere the visitors were able to admire scenes and sculptures that continue to fascinate and delight tourists almost a century later:

After the tombs we rode back to where Aboud our guide had lunch laid out for us in the Temple of Thothmes III. These temples are of 18th and 20th Dynasties and Ptolemaic work – here one sees the sunk bas-relief and the raised . . . the hieroglyphics are wonderful, you see Rameses going out to battle in his chariot with his pet lion, you see him holding his captives by their hair and cutting their heads off and his soldiers counting the hands and tongues of captives who had insulted his gods.

Then as now, tourists were subjected to continuous harassment by would-be souvenir sellers, offering gruesome fragments of ancient mummies, beads, scarabs and pieces of mummy cloth. For the price of a shilling, Kenneth managed to buy these off before the party made their way back to the hotel. Wherever he went he drew quick sketches in remarkable detail – here a hieroglyph depicting a vulture, there the round tombs of an 800-year-old Coptic cemetery, as well as sketches of the local inhabitants and their curious headdresses.

The tour continued with a visit to Philae:

. . . via our friends the Bisharians. These Bisharians are very probably Kipling's 'Fuzzy Wuzzy', the men's hair stands up on top and down the side and the women's hair is all plaited in castor oil, very small plaits – and oh how they do beg, they run after you for half a mile begging for half a piastre (a penny farthing). They are the camel breeders of Egypt . . . I forgot to tell you that in the Rameses quarries we saw a huge obelisk that had been dressed on three sides, but never cut from its bed. In many places one can see the wedge marks on the rocks still. Holes were drilled and wooden pegs put in, which were then watered, when they swelled and split off the required piece of granite . . .

The sights and sounds seen by today's tourists at Aswan (or Assouan as it was generally spelt 90 years ago) were very much a major attraction in 1917, as described by Kenneth:

> After tea, Aboudi our guide had a boat waiting for us with Soudanese musicians in the bows with tomtoms and they sang and danced as we rowed to Lord Kitchener's and Elephantine island. These are both beautiful islands, with lovely gardens – on the former I picked a pomegranate, just for the pleasure of picking it off its own tree. On the latter island we saw the ancient Nilometer for measuring the water – this is a passage and staircase leading into the water, on the walls of which are the ancient markings of the Nile . . . we finished up with bright moonlight and the musicians singing away with their peculiar wailing way. They are peculiar chaps and don't give a hang for their audience, they sing to each other – even when we had left them to visit one of the islands, they sang away and were quite happy . . .

On their final day the little party visited the alabaster quarries, from which the former outer covering of the Gizeh pyramids had been cut, before returning to Luxor and catching the overnight train back to Cairo for two nights at Shepheards Hotel: 'waste of time I call it – doing Mameluke tombs, mosques, and pyramids, but I haven't the heart to describe it, after all the wonders of Luxor and Aswan – the trip of a lifetime . . .'

The trip of a lifetime it most certainly had been, for Kenneth, at the very end of this long descriptive letter, running to 19 closely-written pages, chose now to break his most important news to the family at home:

> Well now, to turn to another aspect of the journey . . . I am engaged to one of those 'dear sweet nurses' – no, not on account of Aswan and Luxor and all the lovely surroundings. I met her first when I was in hospital, she was night nurse, and we used to sail together in the evenings. We were just good pals at first and enjoyed the sails, and never thought anything more about it. Then in the middle of February she went to Alexandria on three days' leave and we found we didn't at all appreciate the days alone, so we just had a quiet chat when she came back and I said 'Shall we?' and she said 'Let's' and that's how it started. No, I'm not joking, dear old people, we just love each other like ————————, and we are always saying 'oh why doesn't the war end', for directly I get settled after the war we are going to be married. So, prepare to be grand-parents and aunt in a year or two's time! I am sending a snap or two of her, I will try and beg a decent one to send you. Don't think we shall hurry things, I know I am handicapped to a certain extent, and we have no intention of spoiling our prospects; she is a year older than I am, and we are both being very wise about it. Her name, by the way, is Ellen Franklin and she has just been awarded the Royal Red Cross – which is equivalent to the Military Cross – she got it for a lot of work with diphtheria cases . . . you can think of us on Saturday evenings, we always have dinner together at one of the hotels. All this is strictly private and only for the family . . .

Writing home on 17 April Kenneth felt able to mention the resumption of major fighting – the first Battle of Gaza had actually begun on 26 March but he presumably felt under obligation not to mention this at the time, until it became public knowledge:

There has been a bit of a stunt up the desert lately and we have been kept most awfully busy . . . There was a very amusing thing happened in the 'stunt'; some Australian troopers captured a Turkish field gun and turned it on the Turks who were in some houses. Well, none of the Anzacs knew how to sight a gun, so opened the breech and looked up the barrel until they could see the house, and then loaded and fired – scoring a direct hit at 50 yards. But, the recoil was so great that it knocked them all over. The next shot they lashed the gun to a telegraph pole and the recoil broke it into three pieces. After that they gave up gunnery and galloped off with the gun!

The 'bit of a stunt' was in fact the Second Battle of Gaza, a failure despite the use of a handful of tanks, which fared badly in the desert sands. Only eight of them had been sent out from the Western Front and these were already in poor mechanical condition. General Dobell's plan was based on massive artillery support in the style practised in

Casualties from the fighting in Sinai had to be evacuated, in the absence of roads, by litters on camels. On arrival in the Suez Canal zone they would be assigned to General or 'Stationary' hospitals for treatment. Serious cases went back to Alexandria or the Cairo area or to Malta. Many convalescents went to Cyprus before return to their units in the field.

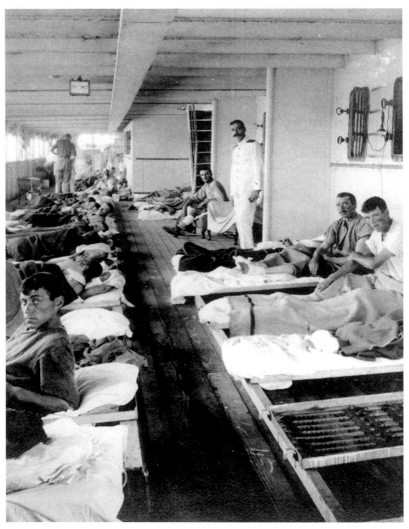

Convalescent ward on the promenade deck of, probably, the *Gascon*. Sister Franklin seems to have served on this ship, from which she could well have been offshore at Gallipoli in 1915, well before KD was posted out to Port Said.

France but he had insufficient guns to produce the stunning barrage demanded. General Murray, who had entrusted Dobell with this second attempt to take Gaza, unaccountably failed to check his plans and GHQ seems to have washed its hands of anything to do with the battle. Dobell's tactics proved no more effective than in the first battle and the attack failed against robust Turkish opposition, with over 6,000 casualties. The wounded were subjected to severe privations during their evacuation, many of them dragged for miles over the sands in sledges pulled by camels. The Turks were well prepared and stubbornly held their ground, and the British staff work was sloppy. As a result there was a cull of the British high command; Murray and his field commander Dobell were replaced and the Egyptian Expeditionary Force was left to ponder its shortcomings, soon to be resolved by the vigour and professionalism of Allenby the new Army commander. Arriving in Egypt in June 1917 he took one look at the state of his command, particularly its depressed morale, and cabled the War Cabinet in London for reinforcements – two more infantry divisions and more artillery. The Cabinet, who had pressed Murray to conduct an offensive into Palestine and were nonplussed by the double failures at Gaza now faced a choice between sitting tight on the Palestine border or reinforcing Allenby with divisions that were equally in demand on the Western Front, thus giving him the means to defeat the Turks and press on to Jerusalem, with the enormous moral force that its capture would represent. Allenby was accordingly given his reinforcements and went ahead with his planning. In the Canal Zone the arrival of yet more troops added to the sense of excitement and optimism. Despite earlier reverses and disappointments there might now be some hope of an early outcome and the defeat of the Turks.

Kenneth continued to work at the Censor's Office with his amiable colleagues, while maintaining his accustomed regime of letter-writing to the family. Having broken the news of his engagement he now felt able to mention his affianced in his letters, usually referring to her not by name but as 'Sister'. She is mentioned thus in a letter dated 30 April 1917:

'Sister', as portrayed by Kenneth, probably in Alexandria, shortly before she sailed for home. All nursing sisters were issued with Panama hats when serving in hot climates. She is also wearing the coveted ribbon of the Royal Red Cross, awarded to her for outstanding work during outbreaks of cholera.

I haven't seen much of Sister lately, she is very busy and won't leave her ward, except for a few moments if I go over. She rushed in to see me the other day with her sleeves rolled up and blood all over her apron, she had been picking bullets out of a man's arm! But never mind, I wouldn't take an ounce of her attention from these poor wounded chaps, they want all the attention they can get. She has one rather special patient, a poor little chap that has lost a leg and arm. He is a Cockney flower seller at home and is rather amusing in his remarks. He doesn't appreciate chicken and champagne but asked for kippers, so I got him some tinned ones, I couldn't get anything else, and he woke one morning to find he had kippers for breakfast . . .

Kenneth's announcement of his engagement naturally came as a great excitement to his parents, who were clearly delighted, and in a letter of 15 May he felt able to tell them all about his fiancée:

Dear old people,

Now for the other part of your letter of the 24th April. I appreciate all you have said about this 'dear sweet Sister' very much, and so does she; she thinks I am very lucky to have such a nice old family. Her father is a rather crusty old gentleman and her mother has been dead some years and I think she is rather looking forward to seeing you all. I am so glad that you like the photos of her that I sent you – everyone admires her, and says what a sweet face she has – all my pals compliment me on my choice. Some of the naval men here who have seen her bring a boat in under sail and stop dead alongside the quay, think she is a marvel (so do I). Well, I could go on talking for ages but I don't want to tire you, except to say that the more we see of one another, the more happy and contented we are.

On the afternoon that this letter was posted Kenneth and his fiancée had an adventure which, though lightly described in the next day's letter home, could well have done for them both; they were caught unawares by the Haboo, the ferocious wind from the western desert bringing with it a dense sandstorm:

I called for her at 2.15 in the afternoon to go for a sail. I had not got my usual felucca as she is on shore being painted so John provided me with another, a nice little boat to sail but rather light.

The sky in the west was terribly black with clouds and I thought a thunderstorm was coming up.

Well, we decided to go up the canal to the Armenian camp so we went down a small canal alongside the harbour, between the coal bunkers. Suddenly I noticed that the wind had changed and what I took to be dense smoke, but which turned out to be sand, and without a moment's warning we were hit such a smack and got the Haboo full force. We had no time to get the sail down or even get the tiller over, to put her up into the wind, and we heeled over and half filled with water. I managed to right her, but only for a second and over we went again. Once more I was able to right her and shouted to some natives in a rowing boat to take Sister off, which they did. Then John and I sat on the side of our sinking ship and tried to keep her afloat while she was driven onto the shore. We drove right on top of another boat and we just managed to scramble into another boat as ours went under. Directly we were sunk I thought of another felucca ahead of me. There was one officer on board and a sick nurse (she had been laid up with a sprained back with lifting Tommies and cannot walk). So I went over to the Seaplane island and borrowed their tug to go and look for them. I found them quite safe, they had kept afloat and got their sail down and were trying to row back. The poor nurse was lying in the bottom of the boat so we lifted her on board and ran her back to hospital as quick as possible. And all the time, Sister was left alone with John salving our ship. But I knew *she* was all right – I have never seen a girl so game, she didn't shriek or cling to me when we were sinking but threw her weight to the right side of the ship – and when she got on shore she laughed and said it was the best afternoon we had had! When I returned from landing the sick nurse an officer on the Seaplane island asked me to come along and have some tea. I thanked him but said I must go over and collect my nurse. 'Oh', he said, ' That's all right, she's here having tea with us.' They had sent across and rowed her over, and given her a wash and brush-up and apologised for not being able to give her a change of clothes!! . . . Well, that's a Haboo, and I never want to see another. People in Port Said have never seen one before.

Best love, dear old people, God bless you all, Ken.

In the same week as this near disaster, Kenneth was reassuring the family at home that he had not entered precipitately into his engagement:

I don't think we have been in a hurry. I have weighed things carefully, and when I was in hospital and she was on night duty (before I ever thought of anything) I used to watch her moving about the ward – she never seemed to make a muck of things or to bungle and she was always calm and collected – and what struck me more than anything, she always had her apron on so neat and square. Then one day I asked her to go for a sail . . . it was company for me and she was a good pal to talk to . . . well, I taught her to sail, and when I came out of hospital she used to bring the boat over to Port Said for me, and 'pon my soul I was proud to get into the boat and sail off with such a girl – this to my mind shows capability and common sense . . . As regards my engagement being known, I really don't know what to say – it is my future I am thinking of – you see, I am done as regards my old profes-sion and am more or less reckoning on Uncle Dick's promise to me [a generous portion of his wealth] or what I can hammer out of the War Office myself – and so I don't want Uncle D. to say I am a fool and should have waited – what do you think about this? . . . well, leave it to you entirely, if you think he will take to it kindly – tell him by all means.

Dear Mother o' mine – I know I am handicapped and what it may mean, but it doesn't worry me in the least – have you ever seen me worried over it?!! If I hadn't lost my arm I would never have met the dear sweet nurse ('Dog-eyes' I call her, but you mustn't tell anyone, she has such sweet eyes, they are like a dog's, when he puts his head on your knee and looks up . . .).

The U-boat campaign in the Aegean and Mediterranean continued to inflict serious losses on Allied shipping, and belated steps were taken to impose a convoy system to safeguard ships bringing supplies and reinforcements from the United Kingdom, and the equally important ammunition ships on the Marseilles-Egypt route. Kenneth gloomily reported, in a letter home on 20 May, that all mail posted in England between 27 and 29 April had gone down. He also described an unusually vicious dust storm that hit Port Said on 19 May:

> Yesterday the wind shifted round to the east and it blew a dreadful Khamseen. I have never seen such a bad one, the air was thick with fine sand, and we couldn't see across the harbour, in fact it was just like a yellow fog and every mortal thing in the house is covered with dust . . .

Whenever time permitted Kenneth crossed over the canal to be with his fiancée (explaining that she lived in Sinai while he was in Lower Egypt) and they drove along the Sinai bank of the canal indulging in an unusual pastime:

> Sister and I have invented a new form of sport. We shoot land crabs with my .22 pistol. She is very funny, as we are going

along she says, 'You know, I think it's rather cruel to shoot them' then when we see some she says 'Look, there's a bunch, give me the pistol' and bang goes a bullet – 'oh – I've hit one, look at him running round!' and she's as pleased as Punch.

Although he seldom mentioned his former service in France and Flanders Kenneth nevertheless thought a lot about his old battalion the 1st/4th Leicesters, and rejoiced whenever a chance encounter enabled him to catch up on events; writing home in June 1917 he describes 'two jolly surprises':

This last week on Friday an air mechanic came up to me in the street and said, 'Excuse me Sir, aren't you Mr Dalgliesh?' and there standing in front of me was a very old pal of mine called Deakin. I was so glad to see him, he comes round to drinks whenever he can and is so pleased for a little civilisation – he has been out on the east coast of Africa for months and is cooped up in a ship in the harbour. The next day, Saturday I ran into Lieutenant Kirk of my own battalion. He has been out here in the Air Service for several months, and is now on his way home, preparatory to going to France. He has been in to several meals and we've had some fine long chats. I hear my battalion has been 'over the top' again in France and nearly everyone is knocked out . . .

There were many queries from his parents to be answered as they were still agog to find out more about his fiancée:

I didn't know I was being so quiet about my engagement. I'm only too willing to talk about her, but I'd hate to bore you – I feel you always want news of Egypt. I don't know how many brothers and sisters she has got, they are a large family, and she has lost two brothers in France and I think all her sisters are married . . . Her eyes are either grey or green, I'm not sure which as I'm always looking at them – she's got sweet eyes.

She isn't extra tall, about mother's height and her hair is dark
– she always dresses very plainly, but my hat she knows how
to put on her clothes. I really don't know how to describe her,
we are so dreadfully in love with one another that we don't
bother about the small details, we just float along in oblivion
when we are together – oh damn this war, we do so want it
to finish so that I can settle down and we can get married.

I was dreadfully worried about you all when I knew an air
raid had been over Folkestone – and you seem to have had it
over Hythe as well, I'm thankful you are all safe, dear old
people – this damn war is an overrated pastime. As regards
the duration of this b—— war, I shouldn't be surprised if it
finished this coming autumn, if not then, well, next spring. I
can't see how it can last any longer. I don't know what I'm
going to do after the war. I shall not farm with Wayet, he is
a nice chap, but an awful old fool. I shall go and worry the
War Office. I wish I knew I had something definite to go to,
I could then get married now. Ah well, never mind, Mr Officer,
as the Arabs say.

He was greatly comforted in this matter by a letter he received
shortly afterwards from Uncle Dick, wishing him every happiness
in his engagement and ending with the comforting words:

'When you come home, you may rely on the Duke and myself
pushing for a job for you.' So I feel very happy and contented
all round, and Sister and I feel we can more readily settle to
another six months of this banishment.

The new Commander in Chief of the Egyptian Expeditionary
Force wrought a sea-change in the morale and motivation of this
large force comprising troops from the United Kingdom, Australia,
New Zealand and India. Allenby continually toured his command,
making it his business to visit every unit, displaying his formidable
ability to remember the names of officers and soldiers alike. He

insisted that constant training at an intensive level would guarantee success when his army broke the Turkish defences at Gaza and Beersheba. At the same time, any who showed signs of incompetence or neglect of their duties could expect to feel the full force of his terrible temper. Meanwhile another campaign was underway in the Arabian desert where the young Oxford archaeologist and Arabic scholar T.E. Lawrence was raising the Hashemite tribes against the Turkish occupying force. The Hashemites were the hereditary guardians of Islam's holy places and one of them, as Sharif of Mecca in 1914, had defied the Sultan's order as Caliph of all Islam, to declare a *jihad* against the infidel Anglo-French alliance. Because of this the British and French governments had agreed to arm the rebellious tribes and under Lawrence's leadership they were to wage a successful guerrilla campaign against the Turks for the rest of the war.

The revolt had begun on 8 June 1916 and by the middle of the following year Lawrence was about to besiege and capture the key port of Akaba on the Red Sea; it fell to his tribesmen on 8 July 1917. By the end of October Allenby was poised to renew the offensive; on 31 October Beersheba fell, to be followed a week later by decisive victory in the Third Battle of Gaza. A month later Allenby entered Jerusalem, humbly and on foot rather than mounted – an astute political move widely noted with approval in the Arab world.

The steady build-up of the Egyptian Expeditionary Force and the successive demands of campaigns in Egypt, on the Gallipoli peninsula, the Dardanelles, Salonika and Palestine, laid heavy burdens on the Army medical services. Between April 1915 when the Gallipoli campaign began, and its conclusion in January 1916, the number of hospital beds required in Egypt increased from 3,500 to some 36,000 and over 104,000 casualties passed through them. To meet this increase the Egyptian government offered the use of its civil hospitals, and many public buildings and hotels were requisitioned as emergency hospitals. Most of the luxury hotels up the Nile as far south as Aswan were taken over as convalescent homes. In this way it was intended that evacuation to the United Kingdom, with the consequent permanent loss of manpower subsequently diverted to the Western Front, would be avoided, and the less seriously wounded and sick cases returned to the fighting line in Palestine. By the middle of 1916, under the supervision of the Surgeon General at GHQ in Egypt, three British, two Australian and three Canadian base hospitals were functioning; in addition there were six British and three Australian and New Zealand general hospitals, several of which were to be found in and around the Canal Zone. With intensification of the fighting in Palestine in the autumn of 1917 as Allenby's advance gained momentum the workload on Sister Franklin and the other Army nurses was further increased.

The prospect of marriage had turned Kenneth's mind to his own financial position which, thanks to the promise of generous backing from Uncle Dick, was sound. In a letter home of 23 August he noted that he had a holding of £500 with the Bank of England, 'a nice nest-egg to have when one contemplates matrimony'. He was also determined to see that he received his due pension rights when he was demobilised and asked his parents to buy the *Army and Navy Gazette* for 21 June 1917 to check the matter of officers' pensions: 'I think I am entitled to more money. I reckon I ought to get £140 or £122 per annum . . . I reckon I am totally disabled for my old profession . . .'

Boredom was a constant problem in a confined garrison such as Port Said, particularly when 'Sister' was fully occupied in the hard-pressed hospital:

I believe people would train performing fleas out here for something to do. Up the desert they keep tarantula spiders and make them fight – they have brigade champions even . . . we go out and net fishes by putting a net round and hauling in to the shore and I take my tunic off and thoroughly enjoy myself and Sister and I enjoy it and row a boat about and she gets as excited as anyone. The first afternoon we got about 1.5 cwt of fish, the three biggest being 5, 9, and 13 lbs – all bass.

In August 1917 Kenneth was promoted:

Dear old people,

Thank you for your letter of congratulation ... I can't tell you exactly how pleased I am, but I think I know how pleased you all are. I did so want my Captaincy and now I have got it I don't altogether care if they do discharge me at the end of the war, I shall at least go as a Captain. Sister is delighted and calls me 'old three stars'. I wrote her a note telling her to be sure and be quite punctual next afternoon as I had something very important to show her (warning her that it wasn't a Military Cross!). She turned up on the tick of time and it was about three minutes before she spotted it. I'd got 'em up you bet, I had 'em on the same evening I got your letter. I got three other letters by that mail addressed to Capt. D. . . . well, my day of jubilation here was brought to rather an abrupt close. Sister and I were up the canal and had tied up for tea. After tea she said she felt sick, so we landed and the poor little beggar 'catted' her heart out. On the way back she fed the fishes again and when we reached the Armenian camp she begged me to take her ashore. So I took her to the hospital there and we had to put her to bed. She had diaroea (damn the spelling) and sickness every few minutes. I phoned to the Matron and she sent up a launch with MO and Sister on board and we took her back on a stretcher ... it was a touch of ptomaine poisoning. I phoned thro' yesterday morning and found she was a bit better and in the evening when I saw her she was quite bright but considerably played out. I had a note from her this morning and she is almost right and hopes to be on duty again in a day or two ... I have always thought she was the sweetest thing on earth, but when I saw her last night with her hair in two big 'plaits' and her dear white arms, I nearly ate her all up!

'Sister' made a good recovery and Kenneth was soon writing home, unrestrainedly extolling her virtues:

Sister is dearer to me every day, and we just love one another with all our hearts and souls – I was standing on the balcony last night looking out across the harbour and thinking of you all and this dear sweet woman, and I thought how perfect it is to be so loved and to love so absolutely in return – there's not a thing to mar our happiness at present – tho' of course we shall have our troubles and worries in the future, but we can face them together – oh I mustn't go on blathering like this to you, but I do want to show her to you so much, for I know you'll love her as much as I do. She is practically all right again after that dreadful ptomaine poisoning – the doctor thought the other one was going to die once – I'm so thankful that dear old Dog-eyes is alright. It pulled her down very much but I've sent her some Burgundy and that ought to pull her together again.

Despite this tonic, 'Sister' was so run down from the effects of the food poisoning that she was sent off to Alexandria and Kenneth's morale suffered accordingly; he was pessimistic about his future as an architect and considered applying for the extension of his commission after the war in order to continue in the Army as Adjutant of a Territorial unit:

I tell you, Sister and I are going to get married pretty soon after we come home – Dam the B———y war, we are both over 30. I like that Adjutant idea better than anything else – you see architecture is knocked on the head and having spent three years soldiering, why not carry on with it, if I don't it means starting to learn something else . . .

To add to his despondency, his colleagues were beginning to leave the Censor's Office. John Kerr, whose amputation had begun to give trouble, had been sent home for further treatment:

Well, John Kerr has gone home, he left on the 4th and now Wayet and I are running the show between us. I miss old John very much, we used to curse one another at times but he was a good old scout and I hated his going away. I am boss of the office – both offices – now and am thoroughly enjoying it – Wayet is a fathead and hasn't the courage of his convictions so I took over the wheel and I fairly put the breeze up him sometimes. I do all the correspondence and the directing of operations and I just love it, only the days just aren't long enough . . .

That was at the end of September, but Kenneth had become run down without realising it, and was sent off from Port Said to GHQ at the beginning of the next month, ostensibly on 'light duty' but in fact on leave, accommodated at the Bulkeley Casino Hotel in Ramleh, near Alexandria and close to GHQ. He was naturally delighted to discover that 'Sister' was staying close at hand for part of her convalescent leave, two minutes' walk away from his hotel, and that she had been instrumental in obtaining a room for him at the Bulkeley Casino:

I spend the mornings on the beach with her, in my shirt, trousers and my head in her lap – and altogether we are having a lovely 'honeymoon'. I sleep most of the afternoon then we go into Alex for tea and come back here for dinner. She's getting stronger and well again and plumper – I know she's getting plump because I smacked her today!

Refreshed by their holiday Kenneth and 'Sister' returned to work at Port Said where he found a new flatmate:

Well, Paterson has left me, he's gone home to England and I have a Lieutenant Hebeler, RN (known as Brassface) living with me now. He is a rum old stick, he has sailed before the mast and fought in the Mexican war, sunk a submarine, helped in the bringing down of a Zepp etc. etc. He is a queer tempered chap (but then I am too, I ought to be ashamed to admit it!)

but we have always got on well and I think that as long as we leave each other alone, we will get on all right. I hate to be bothered and so does he ...

Writing home in the last week of October Kenneth made no mention of the major battles in progress as Allenby came to grips with the Turks at Gaza and Beersheba, other than a veiled reference to the heavy workload in the Port Said military hospitals; he had, however, plenty to write about to his parents who had at last written to his fiancée and welcomed her into the Dalgliesh family:

Thank you so much for your dear sweet letter to Sister ... she loved your letter and will be writing soon, perhaps really not for a little while as they are busy and I take all her spare time! You ask me what you are to call her – well I'm blest if I know. We both agree that her two Christian names are quite impossible, they have been a worry to her all her life – just fancy 'Constance Ellen'!!! Her own sisters and brothers call her Nell, and others call her Jane or Janie so if you don't like those you must invent a name for her. I call her Dog-eyes meself, but then you see that's private property.

Yes, that little house in the country that you have imagined is quite our idea. It's going to be a small cottage and we are going to keep a pig so that I can lean over the style on Sunday mornings & scratch his back; we are going to grow all our own vegetables and have nice old-fashioned flowers. Oh I do hope that all we think and talk about will come true ...

I forgot to tell you that when I was at Alex I went for a flight in an aeroplane; it was 'great', we flew right over Aboukir Point and saw the bay. We were about 1,000 feet up and doing about 70 miles per hour. The sea looks lovely from such a height – no more now,

Best love dear old people, God bless you all, Ken.

Port Said had little to offer in the way of entertainment, but strenuous efforts were made to occupy the troops, and in particular to divert them from the joys and resultant perils of the red light district when off duty. Kenneth was appointed President of the Garrison Entertainments Committee and he tackled his responsibilities energetically; writing on 17 November he described his first effort at mass entertainment:

> I got a lot of Japanese to give a display of jujitsu, one show at the camp and one at the hospital. It was one of the finest jujitsu displays I have ever seen – they chucked each other over their heads nearly every time. At the hospital I got one of the Sergeants to take on one of the Japs with boxing gloves . . . it was most interesting to watch the difference between the two arts. Last night I organised a free concert for the men at the local cinema hall which was also a great success. I had a full band there and several comedians and a ventriloquist. We sold the boxes for 5/- each to officers and the hall was free to the men. During the evening there was a lovely scrap on the stairs between a big black West Indian and all and sundry around him. He butted one man under the chin . . .

Kenneth's production of the Japanese martial arts team was a considerable achievement. He had discovered the presence in the eastern Mediterranean of a Japanese naval force as part of the allied anti-submarine campaign and its personnel gladly offered their somewhat exotic services for the entertainment of the troops.

In the same letter he relaxed his Censor's role, commenting on news of the Third Battle of Gaza and Allenby's decisive victory:

> Well, what do you think of the news from this front – pretty good eh? I have seen thousands of prisoners. I enclose some photos. They are a dirty crowd and as lousy as cuckoos. Directly they march to the prisoners' cage their clothing is baked and

they are put through a creosol bath, and they fight like wild
beasts when the food is served out.

A replacement Censor had joined the team in November – a Second
Lieutenant Fricker who, newly commissioned and not in receipt of
staff pay, could not afford to live in the flat. Kenneth acquired a
tent for him to save expense and drew his rations, feeding Fricker
at the flat and charging him a nominal amount for this; the arrange-
ment clearly worked happily and the three officers got on well enough
to throw dinner parties to which 'Sister' and some of her colleagues
were invited. As she was on night duty over Christmas 1917 the
celebrations were somewhat muted, but Kenneth was taken aback
on Christmas Eve when, on entering the flat's kitchen to give the
cook his orders, he came across two live fowl in a crate and a turkey
walking around the floor as the cook threw handfuls of corn to the
birds. Later in the week 'Sister' held a dinner party at the flat for
its occupants and several of the nursing sisters:

> Really, my cook excelled, I have never sat down to a better
> dinner: giblet soup, fish, chicken, plum pudding and brandy
> sauce, savoury and dessert. Pommard, Benedictine and coffee
> . . . after dinner we all became tomboys – we sat on the floor
> and played hunt the slipper and kissed all the girls – we played
> musical chairs – Jimmy crawled under the carpet and said he
> was a tunnelling company at work – it was the rowdiest evening
> I have ever had.

Until November, Kenneth and his flatmates had been allotted two
British soldier servants as batmen, but they had become increas-
ingly idle and insolent, so were dismissed and returned to their units.
In their place came two Sudanese:

> . . . two very good boys and such a welcome change to the
> two batmen. Ibrahim shouts out 'Tahib' (yes Sir) and runs
> round the table when he is serving dinner. He always does

everything at the trot. The floors are polished and everything is sweet and clean. They are both very amused at our attempts at Arabic and usually have a broad grin on their faces . . . the concerts are still going strong. I have run two free ones in Port Said and two over at the 31st hospital. Next Wednesday I am running one in one of the wards for the very sick men . . . I have great difficulty with the cinema people, they are Greeks and d—— swine to deal with but if I have any trouble I go round to the base commander (Percy) and get him to write them a letter or I should say *I* write the letter and he signs it (which is often more effective). No – I don't have to take the chair at these shows but I frequently have to make a speech. Sister roars with laughter when I make speeches.

'John Sullivan', Kenneth's boatman, was no longer in evidence:

. . . seems to have gone to the dogs – like most Arabs. He used to turn up late or not at all and was always worrying me to get him passes or bail him out of the caracole [police station] and now we haven't seen him for ages – I think he must have become a fisherman. Sister and I haven't done much sailing since she has been on night duty. She only gets a little time in the mornings to come to me and goes on in the evening again . . . we both say *damn* night duty. Well never mind, she's done one month of her time now and will resign on the 17th of this month, and then I want her to come home, she's been out here long enough, three seasons in the heat, over three years' active service which for her means practically three years on her feet. She is wonderful with her work, the patients all think so much of her – one poor chap thanked her before he died for all her kindnesses – I don't know how she sticks it – and the barrack life they have to live, she wants her own little house so much & so do I.

You ask what her interests are, they are the same as mine, we are always happy doing the same thing – she likes the same things I like and that's why I know old mother especially will love her because she and I also like the same things. You know, you can't expect a nurse to have many interests developed. Sister has been doing nothing but nursing for the last ten years, and living in nursing quarters with damn little money. £20 a year doesn't give one much chance to do anything and she never asked her father for any – poor old girl she used to sell her things instead.

Change was in the air with the new year. On 23 January 1918 Kenneth was confiding his growing weariness in a letter home to his father, whom he addressed informally as 'Jerry':

Dear old Jerry,

It will soon be your birthday and I haven't written to wish you many happy returns of the day – however, do so now with all my heart, you dear old pal. Draw £1 out of my a/c and get yourself a pipe and I also want you to get a small 2/- book called 'The Book of Artemas' published by 'W. Westall & Co, 8 Adam St. Adelphi, WC 2' – the change you are to give to old mother. This book is written like the New Testament, & is a very fine story of the war. I know mother will like it.

Well now, for the great news – Sister is coming home. The hospital leaves here tomorrow and she must go to Cairo and there await a hospital ship which will take her to Marseilles and then across country home. I don't mind telling you, Jerry, my heart is as heavy as lead – I feel like I used to feel when the holidays were nearing their end & I had to go away to school again and leave you all.

She is bringing a lot of stuff with her, brass trays, and a cloak (Bernouse) for mother. Her home address is Morna House, Portchester, Hants. She is dreadfully nervous about meeting all you dear old people – she seems to think you will expect so much . . . She isn't a bit well, & wants a rest badly – I want her to take at least six weeks' holiday. I think you had better write to her, one of you.

I am trying to get home before the summer & have written GHQ asking for an exchange on the grounds that last summer knocked me up and also that I want to get married. My chief has written me a very nice letter saying 'I think that your transfer to England can only be arranged on medical certificate, however, I am seeing what can be done about it'.

A week later Kenneth was back in hospital with:

a d—— great boil as big as Hill 60 on my thigh, which being very high up I can hardly walk. It's nothing to worry about and I am very well treated – but I keep on looking at the door and wondering why my Dog-eyes doesn't come in . . . I am not a bit worried over the Western Front, I have the utmost faith – in fact I always say that it is an Englishman's *duty* to be optimistic. I think that a pessimist ought to be kicked for lack of faith in his own country. As you may imagine I know that bit of ground around Kemmel rather well – it's as clear in my mind as if I had been there yesterday . . .

At that point in the war on the Western Front the appalling battles known as 'Third Ypres' had ended as a bloody morass in which thousands of lives had been lost on both sides; but for the time being the line had stabilised. Elsewhere, the French Army was recovering, albeit slowly, from widespread mutinies following its abortive offensive in 1917, and the Russian Revolution was in full swing on the Eastern Front, with the consequent elimination of Russia from the western alliance. Although Kenneth might have thought his parents pessimistic over the outcome of the war, there was worse to come, as the Germans were already well advanced in plans for their onslaught against the British 5th Army in March 1918, and this would certainly give grounds for misgivings throughout the

United Kingdom when the blow fell. In Palestine, Allenby's advance beyond Jerusalem had been delayed by appalling weather but resumed in mid-February with the capture of Jericho.

Meanwhile, despite a recurrence of his Nile boils, Kenneth was able to be reunited briefly with 'Sister' as described in a letter home on 9 February:

Well now, Sister and all the hospital left Port Said on Jan 24th. I travelled up as far as Ismailia with her and we lunched together on the train. The next morning I got a wire from her to say she had three days' leave so I bolted off to Cairo arriving there at 5 p.m. She met me at the station. All the Sisters were refused dinner leave for some daft notion or other so she took it without asking and in order that we might not be discovered we adjourned nightly to a small restaurant near the Continental Hotel, called St James's and fed jolly well, with no need to dress for dinner – and so did the bally Matron in the eye! One day we went to the races and picked three winners running but the odds were so small we hardly won a cent. We spent no end of our time in the bazaar, sitting outside the small shops drinking Persian tea, smoking Amber cigarettes and bargaining with the natives. We took no guide and so I had to talk my best Arabic! In one shop Sister bought some pure essence scent and the man said, 'Now I will give Sister this small bottle as a present,' so she said, 'Yes, but what are you going to put in it?' 'I will give you any scent you like.' So she promptly chose the most expensive, and the bottle held about 10/- worth! In the amber bazaar I got a large amber bead and a small piece, then we went to a silk bazaar and had a big purple silk cord and tassel made, and now it's a most delightful necklace. It will look awfully nice on a white silk blouse . . . Another day we went into a large workshop where all the fake furniture, doors, table, trays and lamps etc. are made. It was an eye-opener I can tell you – & everything so beautifully made . . . Sister is bringing home 100 Amber cigarettes that I got.

They are the celebrated eastern cigarettes but one must not smoke more than one or two a week or your nerves will soon be all to pieces. Just keep them for very special occasions. Well, I returned to Port Said on Monday evening, January 28th, both of us having taken an extra day's leave! We didn't dare to say 'goodbye' on the station. She drove down with me, and when we got to the station yard I kissed her and hopped out, it was too dreadful. And there she is in Cairo and I am here and I don't suppose I'll see her again until we meet in England. She is now waiting for a hospital ship. If one doesn't run soon I fear she will have to go home P&O, as her time is up on the 17th of this month. I do hope the Matron will let her stay on a little while and wait for a HS but we are very much afraid – the Matron is such a bitch and has no consideration or feelings for anyone.

At the end of February, 'Sister' was still stranded in Cairo awaiting her sea passage home, much to Kenneth's frustration. He passed the time with an expedition to Suez at the far end of the canal; having seen the place, he expressed no wish to return, and continued to pine for home and his fiancée:

. . . I am alone now. I had a letter from Sister this afternoon to say she expects to sail today (27 February) and now I realise, mother dear, what you have felt when I have been at sea. I pray God to take my darling safely home. If I can get home myself I am going to do so, I have been meaning to for a long while, the summer is very trying and I've been out here for 17 months now – and I feel there are as good jobs going in England as here. Directly I get home Dog-eyes and I are going to get married, we have settled that long ago. I don't want her to have to nurse again and even if I don't get another staff job I shall have £450 per annum, so I don't see the sense of waiting till after the war – who knows when the war is going to finish.

A week into March, 'Sister' was still delayed in Cairo; Kenneth was becoming more philosophic about their separation, as he wrote home on the 7th of the month:

> I expect she will be away before long now. I am getting used to Port Said without her – more or less, but the day seems to go all wrong and the sun doesn't shine if I don't get a letter every morning. On Saturday she is going to receive her Royal Red Cross from the Duke of Connaught. I wish I could be there to see her.

At the end of the month a highly relieved Kenneth was able to report that he had received a cable from 'Sister', who had arrived safely back in England. He was also diverted and amused by the military bureaucracy that ensued from a GHQ order '. . . that in future all officers and men will stand to attention when the Egyptian National Anthem is played'. He therefore took what he assumed was the appropriate action in his department, writing to the Staff Captain asking that in order that the base Censor's staff could comply with Base Command Order No. — dated 26 March 1918 'may we be supplied with a copy of the Egyptian National Anthem as we have no knowledge of it'. This memorandum was hastily passed onto the Army Service Corps who replied that music was not in their department and suggested that the matter be referred to the Egyptian Labour Corps with a request that one of their men could teach the General Staff the words and music:

> Since then I've heard nothing more!!! And so we amuse ourselves in this rotten world of sin and sunshine. I have a new chief at GHQ now, he's coming down to see me on April 1st. I shall have to give him a good dinner!

Probably symptomatic of his run-down physical condition, Kenneth's plague of boils returned with a vengeance and he went back into hospital. There is a gap in the correspondence at this stage, possibly caused by the loss at sea of a series of mail ships to submarine attack. At this point the war had reached a climactic and crucial stage with the launch of the great German attack on the Western Front. Attacking in dense fog on 21 March the Germans overwhelmed the British 5th Army and the Allied line recoiled. So desperate was the situation after three unrelenting weeks of the offensive that Field Marshal Haig issued his celebrated Order of the Day on 12 April: 'Every position must be held to the last; there must be no retirement. With our backs to the wall, and believing in the justice of our cause, each one of us must fight on to the end.'

By the time Kenneth's letters resumed on 11 May the crisis had passed in France and although the issue remained in the balance for several more weeks, the line held and Haig prepared for the master stroke that would result in the greatest victories ever won by British arms, in the late summer and autumn of 1918. In Palestine, Allenby's force had been drastically reduced by the need to reinforce the Western Front but this did not stop him gaining a final decisive victory over the Turks. The war was entering its final stages and Kenneth, whose work at Port Said was finished, was a passive spectator from a hospital bed in Cairo:

Dear old people,

I have left the Australian hospital at Port Said as they wanted my bed for an Anzac and I have come to the Citadel Hospital in Cairo. It's fine here and the food is fine; it was damnable at the other place. This hospital was Mohammed Ali's Palace and is a most magnificent place – we are perched on a hill (the Citadel) with the Mohammed Ali Mosque alongside (this is the mosque that somewhat resembles St Sophia Constantinople) . . . My boils are getting on very well; I have had two large ones on my thigh and was quite unable to walk for several days . . . I don't suppose I shall be here for many days but it's great to be in Cairo without hotel expenses and be able to prowl around every day from 2 p.m. to 7 p.m. I have found

Inner Courtyard & Tomb, Sulieman Pacha Mosque 22 5/8

One of Kenneth's many memorable pictures of a mosque in Egypt. His fascination with Arabic calligraphy is evident

146

my old friend Mohammed Aboudi (he was my dragoman at Luxor) and I am going for a walk with him round old Cairo this afternoon . . . there are hosts of things I want to see and find out. I have asked Aboudi to take me to a Sheikh's house so that I can see the domestic side of their lives.

A day later Kenneth was eagerly describing his tour of the old city with Aboudi: he was still fascinated by Arabic calligraphy and deter-mined to take some books back home. After a successful visit to the booksellers' bazaar Aboudi was able to obtain two at a cost of 30/-. He was also intrigued by the folklore and customs of the locals and his attitude towards the Egyptians was much changed since his arrival in the country:

. . . we watched people at the Zuwahleh Gate tying pieces of cloth and hair to the iron-studded door and touching it with their hands and then kissing their hands and generally invoking the saint to curse their enemies or help their friends. The saint is supposed to live in a small hole behind one of the large doors. The remains of his turban are still hanging up on the gate (600 years old). We visited the El Azar University where one may see almost every tribe of Arab sitting learning his Koran – they live there for five years. A great many of them sit on a skin rug (sheep and goat skins) and Aboudi told me that if a man habit-ually sits on one for four or five years he will never have any desire for the opposite sex – he said he himself sat on one for a fortnight and found this to be so (I don't think his was a fair test!) . . . Today we are going to call on the Imam of the Mosque by the Zuwahleh Gate. He gets about £7 per month, but in his spare time he writes books and examines scholars from Al Azar University. We are also going to try and find a negro doctor who works charms and uses a similar book to the one I have obtained.

Kenneth's boils continued to give trouble, this being an age without antibiotics, in a climate that positively encouraged infections of all

Lieut. F. Hallam R.N.V.R.

21.1.18.

'. . . if not, I shall have to get my old pal Frank Hallam to do the job, as he knows Ellen very well ...'

sorts. The last of his letters from Egypt to survive is dated 2 June 1918, mentioning his continued hospitalisation and the persistence of his Nile boils:

> . . . but I have now got the bandages off my leg and they are drying up and I'm feeling heaps better . . . so glad you have been getting some of my letters . . . Really, the question of inviting people to one's wedding is a very difficult problem. I thought if no one was invited, no one would be offended – and yet I wanted very much to have Uncle Dick there, but I couldn't ask him without Uncle Frank – and then all the relations would have to come pouring in. I shall have to talk it over with my Dog-eyes and see what she thinks – I expect it will end by everyone being there. Marc is going to be my 'best man' and I expect Ellen's father will give her away, that is if he is in a good humour. If not I shall have to get my old pal Frank Hallam to do the job, he knows Ellen very well.

Once back in England, and with only a few months to serve before his early release from the army, Kenneth served with a reserve battalion of the Leicesters near Lincoln. A soon as the administrative procedures had been completed, he was once again a civilian, eager to make a new life and, if possible, to resume his profession. He had served for just over four years as an officer and little suspected that in little more than twenty years, he would once more be in uniform.

9

AFTERMATH

Kenneth and Ellen were married in London in July 1918 on his return from Egypt, and set up their first home in a small flat in East Finchley while he returned to the architect's profession in which he was to achieve distinction. He never forgot that first home of the life he was to share with his bride:

> . . . there will never be another flat quite like that. The sitting room was an unusual shape but it furnished beautifully, and every night when I went to bed I used to turn at the door and have one last look before I switched out the light . . .

Strong family ties held the Dalglieshes together from generation to generation. Kenneth's father, Theodore Irving Dalgliesh, the Royal Engraver, although regarded as a delicate child, survived to the age of 86. Having started his education at a boarding school in Leicester (which he hated) before serving his apprenticeship to an iron-founder, he discovered his artistic talent when put to work in the drawing office. On completion of this phase of his life he had made his way to London, determined to make his living as an artist, and studied in South Kensington, eventually becoming headmaster of the Nottingham School of Art. Later the family moved to Folkestone and during the war of 1914–1918 they were at Hythe before moving with their daughter to Grasse in the Alpes Maritimes where Theodore's wife died. He came back to England on the eve of war in 1939 and finally settled in a property at Atherstone in Warwickshire where he died in 1942.

The loss of Kenneth's left arm seldom troubled him. He played a good round of golf and enjoyed a full life. After his demobilisation he worked initially as a district architect for the Ministry of Agriculture and Fisheries before setting himself up in private practice. The business thrived in the 1920s and 1930s and the flat which Kenneth and Ellen loved soon became too small. In 1923 they moved to Sidcup where Kenneth designed and supervised the construction of the family home, as well as two other houses in nearby Knoll Road. The family was increasing: Elizabeth had been born in 1920, David in 1922 and Jean, Diana and Robin followed. Ellen, as one of 12 children in her family, had no problems in rearing this new generation. Kenneth's professional reputation grew in the Sidcup and Bexley area and a major enterprise there after building his own home was the design of a project in nearby Old Forge Way. This was a carefully planned estate of homes built in the style of seventeenth- and eighteenth-century cottages of the Kentish Weald, described in 1988 by the planning authority of Bexley Borough Council as '. . . an exceptionally fine example of a cottage estate . . . using a range of traditional materials. The design and detailing belies the estate's 1936 origin'. The entire estate, comprising some 20 residences, has been designated a Conservation Area.

Apart from the Old Forge Way project, a number of pubs, and the design of Waring Park – previously the property of Lord Waring but now a public park, Kenneth's greatest architectural legacy, designed in partnership with Roger Pullen ARIBA, is the art deco Marine Court development at St Leonard's on Sea, for which the foundation stone was laid in 1936 and which now enjoys English Heritage Class II listing. Its foundation stone was laid by Mr R. Holland-Martin, Chairman of Southern Railways. The building, at that time the tallest block of flats in the country, consisted of 153 sets of apartments, three restaurants, a basement car park, 20 shops at street level and a promenade deck on the 13th floor. It had to be built on a narrow site and Kenneth Dalgliesh and his associates based the design on that of one of the great Cunard liners that he had greatly admired when visiting Southampton. In May 1937 a

Three generations of Dalglieshes: left to right, David (b 1922) in Merchant Taylor's School OTC uniform; Theodore, the former Royal Engraver; Kenneth in his 1914–18 Service Dress uniform; and Robin (b 1930) in front. Kenneth's prominent Captain's rank insignia, worn on the slashed cuff, are those in use before less obvious ones were adopted. Even so, by 1916 many units at the front insisted that junior officers, being the most vulnerable to sniper fire, adopted private soldiers' uniforms bearing unobtrusive rank badges of cloth.

Marine Court, St Leonard's on Sea, KD's impressive design based on a Cunard liner.

competition offering a £5 prize was held to choose a name for the building. Suggestions, many of which must have greatly amused the architect, included 'Sunny South Court', 'Monstrosity Mansions', 'Have no Care House', 'Mammon Court' and 'Controversy Building'. The top six floors were damaged, as was the eastern corner, by bombing in the 1939–45 war but it still stands and is in full use.

Kenneth plunged into local affairs. He became Honorary Architect to Sidcup Cottage Hospital and a respected member of its governing committee, designing its Watts Ward containing the X-ray department and the nurses' accommodation, and in 1937 became President of the hospital. His versatility extended to the design of a memorial stained glass window in Eynsford Parish church and the design and repair of weathervanes – including that at the old Twickenham rugby football ground.

154

Away from his professional work Kenneth became deeply involved in the life of his parish church and in the welfare of war veterans. As a member of the Parochial Church Council of All Saints' Church, Foots Cray, he supervised work on repair of the fabric until the outbreak of war in 1939. For some years he presided over the Sidcup Horticultural Club (the oldest in the country), assisted in the formation of the local Conservative Club, and was an extremely active member of the British Legion and of the Sidcup and District United Services Club, whose President he became in 1950. He continued to play golf until his latter years and even found time to serve as a Special Constable during the General Strike of 1926.

Although his time at the Front in Flanders had been short, Kenneth never forgot the men he had led and remained a member of the Tigers' Regimental Association, attending reunion events from time to time. He ensured that his faithful soldier-servant Private Orton obtained useful employment as an outside railway porter and visited him from time to time during the inter-war years. It was probably on one such visit in 1931 to Leicester, with a few hours to spare, that he determined to see how his old company Sergeant Major was coping with life in post-war England. It proved to be a tragic reunion:

> I found the house, its windows boarded up, in a mean street of terraced homes. I immediately sensed that something was wrong. I knocked on the door and presently it was opened by a woman. I told her who I was and that I had called to see Sergeant Major Bromley. She started to sob and said 'he's dead, come in'. And there in the tiny little front room lay my old friend in his coffin. He had waited for me and I was able to say 'goodbye'. As I stood beside him all the old memories came rushing back, as did my tears, which I was not ashamed to shed . . .

Ellen Dalgliesh never returned to the nursing profession and devoted her energies and skill to bringing up her family; one of her daughters,

Jean, remembers her with great affection as one who 'kept their feet on the ground':

> ... she had five good-looking children. Sitting around the dining room table one tea time one of us made a rude remark about a piano teacher who had a club foot. She said, 'You *never* make fun of anyone with a disability and in the same way, if anyone should *ever* tell you that you're nice looking there's nothing to be pleased about, that's just the way God made you.'

Of Kenneth and Ellen, their daughter recalls:

> They were probably a well-matched pair, he would indulge in wonderful flights of fancy, telling us amazing stories and composing a song for each of us, and she would say, 'Stop filling the children's heads with nonsense', but she provided the basic security and discipline. She offered total security − always knew the answers to any illness or complaint and coped calmly with emergencies.

All three daughters served in the WRNS in the 1939–1945 war; David, as a medical student was exempt from war service but decided to be a naval surgeon and became the medical officer on Sir Vivian Fuchs's Antarctic expedition in 1947, which had to endure two winters there due to the failure of the expedition's ship to reach them. Some years later he himself led an Antarctic expedition, earning him the rare distinction of a Bar to the Polar Medal awarded earlier. Later in his career he became the surgeon on Her Majesty's Royal Yacht *Britannia,* and retired as a Surgeon Commodore having added the Lieutenancy of The Royal Victorian Order and Order of the British Empire to his Polar Medal and Bar to make up a unique set.

He was accompanied to Buckingham Palace for the investiture of his Bar to the Polar Medal by his brother Robin, who had accompanied him on the second Antarctic expedition, the purpose of which had been to establish the Halley Base in advance of the

International Geophysical Year. The Queen was amused and intrigued by this unusual double award and inquired if the Dalgliesh family intended to set up an exploration business in Antarctica.

Kenneth and Ellen shared a love of gardens and theirs at Sidcup was designed by him and maintained by both, with the assistance of their gardener, who became a great friend of the family. Friendship, for which Kenneth had a great capacity, was very important to them both. Holidays were also important and always featured long walks and explorations; the family would long remember damming streams, exploring caves, climbing to summits in the Yorkshire Dales, investigating Dover Castle, fishing from breakwaters (when Kenneth, despite the loss of his left arm, was able to teach the children how to bait their hooks), always broadening their horizons and encouraging them to be full of curiosity. At home, Ellen simply lived for her family, remembered by all of them as a very loving, very understanding and very wise mother. Kenneth's love of sailing endured after the war and all the family enjoyed many voyages across the Channel and along the south coast. He never concealed his pride in the family as they grew up and they reciprocated his affection. At the same time they all recognised his quick temper – a characteristic no doubt inherited from his Uncle Dick – and they learned to respect this. One of his favourite expressions in old age was 'I can't stand other people's children but mine are wonderful!'

Although he had long mastered most daily manual skills the one that eluded him was the tying of shoelaces. The family have affectionate memories of him dashing around the house when late for some appointment, placing a foot on a convenient chair and bellowing for assistance. On the commuter train up to London he was greatly admired by fellow commuters for the dexterity with which he handled a broadsheet newspaper by turning the pages with his teeth whilst keeping his pipe alight. The exemplary manner in which he had overcome what to many would have been a crippling disability was recognised by all who knew him.

With the passage of the years the family grew up and departed to live out their own lives. In old age Kenneth took their departure philosophically, although he missed them terribly, looking back on their happy childhood:

> How completely trusting you were. Those lovely holidays will never come back again; you have grown up, have your own ideas and departed in various directions. You even 'speak a different language' and don't always understand the one we speak – but that is not unusual; the next generation always speaks a different language to the former and always will. There have been weddings and I have experienced those few hallowed moments when everyone has gone ahead to the church and the father is left for a short space of time, completely alone with his daughter; still his own, and he looks at her as she stands in her bridal gown, seemingly more precious than any jewel on earth, knowing he is about to give her to someone else ... 'Who giveth this woman?' and knows she is gone

Kenneth strides out with his sons David (left) and Robin on holiday, c 1937.

beyond recall; but I have been fortunate and been happy in the husbands my daughters have chosen, and so all is well.

On the outbreak of war in September 1939, at the age of 52, Kenneth once more volunteered his services and was commissioned in the

Jean Dalgliesh with her parents on her wedding day to Captain T. M. Braithwaite of the Somerset Light Infantry. Kenneth was now serving as a captain in the Royal Engineers.

159

Royal Engineers in the rank of Captain. Although medically graded as 'Home Service only' this did not prevent him pursuing an energetic career as a camouflage expert, in which his draughtsman's talents were deployed to advantage. One of his major projects was the masking of the great 15-inch coastal guns at Dover. On occasion he was required to go aloft in order to assess the effect of his schemes; taken to task after one sortie in a Lysander Army Co-operation aircraft, he was told to take a parachute on his next flight and duly complied. However, having received no briefing on the use of this device he picked it up by what he imagined was the carrying handle but was in fact the ripcord, with predictable results.

By 1945 Kenneth was demobilised in the rank of Major. He returned to a life given to public service and that of his family. In due course he was elected to Fellowship of the Royal Institute of British Architects and when he died on 11 March 1964, appropriately in Sidcup cottage hospital for which he had worked so long and hard, there were numerous generous tributes from those for and with whom he had worked. His beloved wife survived him for two years.

BIBLIOGRAPHY

It is suggested that I list a short bibliography that may help readers of *Single-handed* to broaden their knowledge of Kenneth Dalgliesh's war: The 4th Leicesters barely merit a mention in the Official History, presumably due to their near obliteration at the Hohenzollern Redoubt in October 1915, so I commend the following as general histories:

Facing Armageddon – the First World War Experience ed. Hugh Cecil and Peter H. Liddle. (Pen & Sword 1996)

The First World War by John Keegan. (Hutchinson/Random House, London, 1998)

The Imperial War Museum Book of the First World War by Malcolm Brown. (Pan Books, London, 2000)

Footprints of the Fourth Leicestershire Regiment by Captain J. Milne. (Privately published)